HISTORIC SUGAR MILLS
IN SANTO DOMINGO

I0866995

The Brian Canin Urban Design Award

HISTORIC SUGAR MILLS IN SANTO DOMINGO

Case Studies in Adaptive Reuse

Jaime Correa & Carmen Guerrero

The Brian Canin Urban Design Award

TABLE OF CONTENTS

PREFACE

INTRODUCTION

GLOBAL PRECEDENTS

Palencia Civic Center, Spain.
Daoíz y Velarde Cultural Center, Spain.
Shelter for Roman Ruins, Switzerland.
Architecture Faculty, Belgium.
Warkteckhof, Switzerland.
Newport Street Gallery, UK.
Highline Housing Project, New York.
Villa Planta, Switzerland.
House of Twenty-Four, Portugal.
Centro Cultural y Musical, Spain.
Museum of Contemporary Art of Rome.
Sagunto Roman Theater Center, Spain.
Slaughterhouse Renovation, Spain.
Centro Cultural y Musical, Dominican Republic.
Kolumba Museum, Germany.
University Hospital, Switzerland.

PROJECT LOCATIONS

PROJECTS

Ingenio Boca de Nigua.
Ingenio Diego Caballero.
Ingenio Palave.
Ingenio Engombe.

ACKNOWLEDGMENTS

CREDITS

PREFACE

LEARNING AS AN EXISTENTIAL ENDEAVOR

Carmen Guerrero

The projects in this pamphlet, a product of the Brian Canin Urban Design Award, are an expression of everything that I have held dear as part of my own Dominican heritage. As a neutral design critic, it was rather difficult to recuse myself from the existential values and the family-shared principles learned over the course of so many yearly visits to the Dominican Republic. As I reflect upon the ideas of historic preservation, afforded by the projects you are about to see, I cannot help but realize that even my own graduate thesis at Cornell University was heavily influenced by the mosaic of the diverse historical styles in the "Zona Colonial" of the City of Santo Domingo – the oldest historic area in the Americas; moreover, the presence of modern tropical buildings, in the midst of the colonial city, is without doubt one of the most impressive collections of the co-existence of modern and pre-modern architectural structures in Latin America and the Caribbean. Therefore, I could not help myself and, under the existential influence of everything that I have experienced over the years, my colleague Jaime Correa and I guided our students to produce projects which would summarize this complex mosaic of existential conditions. The student projects reflect their research findings and their practical applications, but they are also the result of their own existential appreciation of a place with the aesthetic potential to heavily predispose their professional careers and their understanding of the physical world.

When a group of citizens and government officials saw the opportunity to capitalize on the profitable tourism industry of the "all-inclusive hotels," they realized the potential of the historic anthropological order embedded in the material culture of both urban and rural areas all over the country. As a result of a sustained political activism, combined with private investment, the national government began to pay attention to the center of historic cities; the desolation, civil insecurity, and physical decay of the "Zona Colonial" became a thing of the past. This new focus brought about an opportunity to produce adaptive reuse interventions with long term consequences for the preservation of cities and their adjacent rural environments.

I learned about the "Ingenios Coloniales" (Colonial Sugar Mills) when the Director of Patrimonio Monumental, the equivalent to the National Trust for Historic Preservation in the United States, approached us with a proposal to collaborate on a project that had been on their radar for the longest time. Their decision to invest time and money on these historic areas was rationalized as a means to deploy tourists, one of the most important engines in the current economy, along a new route of forced pilgrimage: the hidden web of Ingenios Coloniales. The Ministry of Tourism, together with Patrimonio Monumental, were looking at ways to enrich and bring to the foreground a new tourist route which would focus on the preservation and adaptive reuse of the ruins of some of the most important 15th and 16th century sugar mill complexes in the Americas. I was taken by surprise since my knowledge of the process of sugar production was practically null, and my experience of these ruins had never been a part of my yearly visits to the Dominican Republic. In effect, I had no idea of the dimensions of these ruins nor was I aware that these plantations were so close to the City of Santo Domingo.

As a result of this inquiry, our Brian Canin Urban Design Studio could not stay put, and our decision to collaborate in the production of this worthwhile endeavor became a matter of when and where. At this point, it was just a matter of convincing my colleague Jaime Correa, our sponsors, our Dean, and a selected group of students to embark on this effort: convincing, which took no more than five minutes given the dimension and importance of what we were about to do.

When we started this project, it became transparent that it was very complex to use the word "Dominican" as a qualifier, because being "Dominican" is not a singular qualifier but a very complex state of mind. These categorizations are difficult to apply in a cultural environment where native Indians, African slaves, and Spanish conquistadors co-existed in a sort of melting pot without a real bottom. I had this realization when I studied the history of Dominican Republic during the graduate thesis I mentioned above – in particular the urban and rural history of the North Coast; in this area of the island, the cultural aspects were even more complex, and the colonizers came not only from Spain and its other territories in Africa, including the Canary Islands, but also from many other parts of the world – including a Napoleonic French delegation focused on the settlement of what they thought was an extension of a biblical paradise or the settlement of a vast Lebanese community which is still dominant in urban and rural areas of the country. In addition to all these, and upon the destruction of slavery in the newly formed Republic of Haiti, a lot of French settlers and Haitian former slaves established themselves within the Dominican Republic and enriched the overall character of place and community building with their food, religious beliefs, arts and crafts, and in every aspect of material culture and innovative advancements.

I would like you, the reader, to understand that the Dominican Republic is a very exciting place to work on an architectural project; if architecture is a true reflection of culture, then what particular culture is that we call "Dominican"? And that is precisely the question that gave birth to some of the projects you are about to see. Additionally, and notwithstanding the controversial issues surrounding the preservation of monuments and their adaptive reuse, the student projects in this book capture the essence of a very violent part of the island's history, with tremendous grace, optimism, and elegance.

We encourage you to study these proposals and learn more about the challenges still ahead of us. Our goal, as practitioners and academics, was not to demolish the heritage of Sugar Mills in the Dominican Republic but to admit their timeless value through a re-invention and a re-appropriation of their architectural greatness. We are here advocating a history of recycling and layering by celebrating the existence of rural historic monuments which are currently under the radar but which we know will become among the most important places to visit in the future of the Dominican Republic.

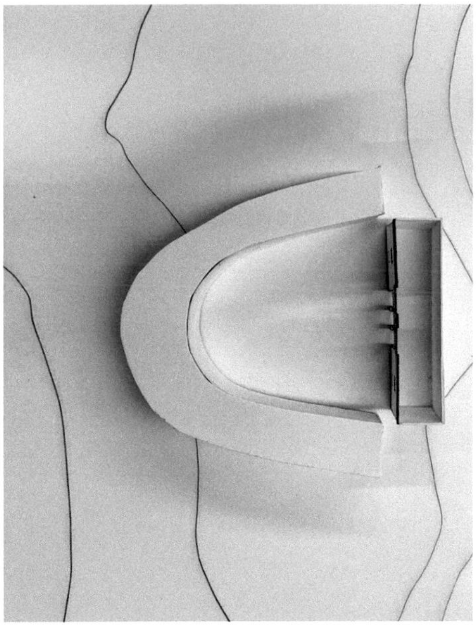
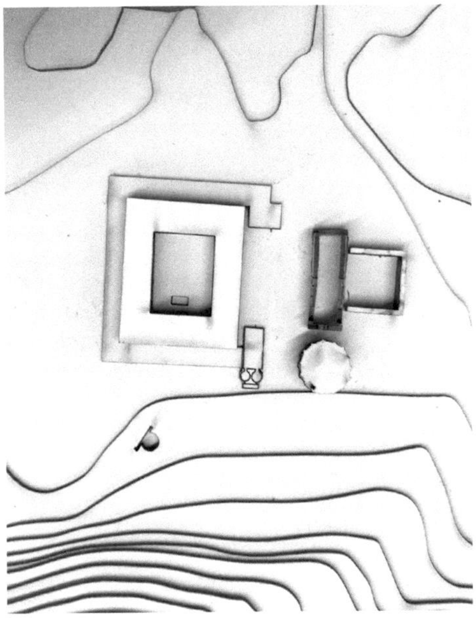

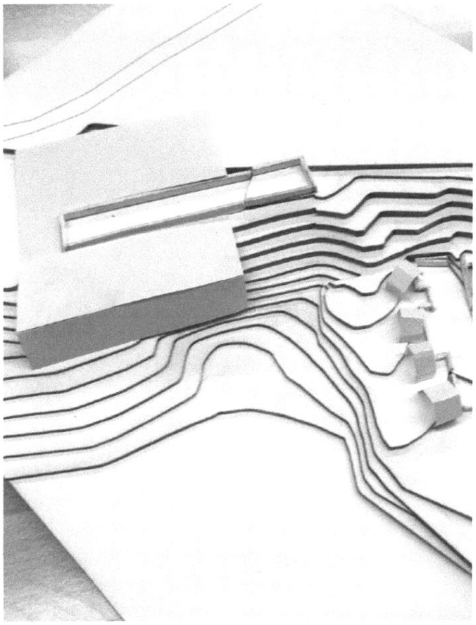

AVOIDING AMNESIA | REMEMBERING DIFFICULTIES
The value of a meaningful context

Jaime Correa

"As Gregor Samsa awoke one morning from uneasy dreams, he found himself transformed in his bed into a gigantic insect."

(*The Metamorphosis*, Franz Kafka)

One of the most famous works of literature of the twentieth century, Frank Kafka's *The Metamorphosis*, begins when the protagonist finds himself transformed into an insect-like creature with numerous legs, a dome-like brown belly, and an armored-plated back. When Gregor Samsa understood that his new condition was not a dream, his bedroom acquired an unfamiliar dimension, his movements demanded a new careful orchestration, and his thoughts were pointlessly uttered in words which nobody could understand. Soon enough, and after a few very painful moments, he realized that when we change, so does our relationship to the world. Since the world in which he lived suddenly became unfamiliar, what used to work no longer did, and problems that did not exist before now did. The old filters were no longer appropriate and, unexpectedly, everything needed to be considered anew.

Gregor Samsa's shift of perspective is what, in the field of psychotherapy, is nowadays called "reframing" – a methodology to approach the same challenges in different ways; through the methodology of reframing, what was once a problem may turn into a new opportunity. The transformative effect of this type of lateral thinking is one in which challenging situations acquire new prospects through a voluntary alteration of the initial conditions. The act of reframing basically changes the patient's patterns of relevance and, consequently, alters the levels of meaning attached to objects or situations.

Similarly, in cities and in architecture, these kinds of metamorphosis and constant reframing are a matter of fact; as inhabitants of urban places and interior spaces, we have no choice but to learn how to adapt to the constant flux of urban development, re-development, and adaptive reuse or to the difficult and unstoppable wrath of the social and physical changes happening in our everyday environment on a regular basis. Unlike Gregor Samsa's unique situation of solitude and immediacy in his own bedroom, cities and architecture are out there in the public realm; they do change and, consequently, so does our relationship to the new world emerging from their multiple transformations.

Lycaon Transformed into a Wolf (1589), engraving by Hendrik Goltzius (1558–1617), Los Angeles County Museum of Art, Los Angeles, CA. Wikimedia Commons.

Reframing does not always work, particularly when we want to avoid difficult situations or painful memories. Just consider the following experiment; what if every morning we could forget the near past and start anew in a world of our own creation? What if we woke up every morning without a memory of where we are or who we are? Or, what if, as in the 1993 movie *Groundhog Day*, our daily experience of the world was obsessively rooted in repetitive routines without a conscious recollection of past events? This is exactly the situation of psychotic patients who after severe trauma forget a portion of their life or fail to recall a difficult memory. In such cases, reframing would be unproductive.

Conscious or unconscious amnesia is even more problematic when difficult social memories are associated with physical elements in our immediate environments, e.g., a tree where someone was unjustly hanged, a statue representing a punishing dictator, a concentration camp, the Berlin Wall, a collective graveyard excavated by authors of human genocide, instruments of torture, an electric chair, the tall boundary walls between white and black American neighborhoods, etc. As cruel as these objects of memory may be, there are definite historic moments that cannot be forgotten; if they are manifested as physical structures, as painful as it might become, they should be kept in perpetuity as moral symbols of unrepeatable acts of repression and human brutality.

The historic sugar mill complexes in the Dominican Republic of colonial times are not immune to this line of thought. Even today, their dilapidated buildings and neglected rural landscapes are still physical containers of very complicated histories of slavery and white supremacy. But, just because they represent painful recollections, should we ignore their important role in the social history of the Island of España? As architects and urban designers, what strategies should we use to exhibit and confront such difficult memories? What kind of values would be achieved by memorializing such a horrific story? Should we just forget this part of history and move on with our present existence? Or, should we use the time-tested role of architecture and urban design to reframe and initiate a process of change that could help us heal and build toward a more just and peaceful future?

Boca de Nigua Sugar Mill Ruins (2019), Dominican Republic. Aerial photo by Luis Felipe Delgado, Copyright © University of Miami, School of Architecture.

The projects in this book are a testament to this epistemological process. Executed with the impeccable design clarity that characterizes the "School of Miami," the adaptive-reuse student projects in the following pages represent both the act of forgetting and the act of remembering.

The group of 16 students participating in the "Brian Canin Family Urban Design Studio" were not so much interested in giving an accurate and truthful reconstruction of past events as in the production of cultural memories that would serve as re-development catalysts and as testimonies for a new beginning. The advantage of treating dilapidated buildings and manipulating neglected rural landscapes as points of departure for re-development is that such adaptive reuse projects avoid the amnesia of abandonment and become meaningful statements that speak to a cultural present while remembering the history of a difficult past.

A preliminary documentation of similar projects around the world brought about questions regarding the implementation of the projects; the main challenge posed, within the context of the studio, was the issue of the pace of implementation of any proposal within a historic environment. Should the implementation of the projects happen in one single sweeping phase? Should interventions be phased gradually to allow the community to get ahold of the potential adaptations of meaning and content? Or, should the projects be left alone to the pragmatic whims and potential informal adaptations and transgressions of residents surrounding these complexes? Answers to these questions are truly difficult in the context of a design studio where the production of a project is the one and only goal for the semester. Nevertheless, because we had the luxury of working within a university environment, this fact did not stop the careful examination of these issues. Regarding the pace of implementation, we were reminded of a quote allegedly recited by Mark Twain: "a round man cannot be expected to fit into a square hole right away. He must have time to modify his shape," thereby meaning that time is of the essence. Upon this realization, the studio moved swiftly into discussions about the gradual transformations of the Diocletian Palace from a place of government luxury to the lively city center of the City of Split, in Yugoslavia, or to the re-appropriations of Roman amphitheaters and Roman circuses in the towns of Lucca and Rome where the elliptical form of the Piazza dell'Anfiteatro in Lucca, or the multiple layers of time-tested functions and forms at the Castel St. Angelo, Teatro di Marcello, and Piazza Navona are among some of the most paradigmatic examples of compatibility in size, character, and shape. These few illustrations of informal and gradual adaptive reuse were extrapolated to the realities of contemporary development practices; soon enough, the students realized that the beauty and mystery surrounding those examples were a part of a unique logistical, functional, cultural, and poetic method difficult to reproduce in contemporary conditions. Instead of transfigurations by trial and error, the students went back to the regular production of immediacy in space-functions compatible with the host sites.

Piazza dell'Anfiteatro, Lucca, Italy (2019), Wikimedia Commons

Teatro di Marcello, Rome, Italy (2018), © Jaime Correa

Castel St'Angelo, Rome, Italy (2018)

Former Mausoleum of Diocletian, Rome, Italy (2018), Getty Images

Diocletian's Palace, Peristyle Court, Split (2019), Wikimedia Commons

The examination of the global situation yielded yet another set of challenges regarding the definition of "good restoration." A careful analysis of contemporary projects proved that the so-called Charter of Venice of 1964, and its intrinsic idea that contemporary projects should not confuse the archaeologists of the future, has had an omnipresent value in most cases. Looking further back in history, students and faculty found that Viollet-le-Duc's quoted definition in his book *On Restoration* of 1785 has been put into contemporary practice almost relentlessly, and without the proper examination of its consequences; it is apparent to the contemporary state of adaptive reuse and re-development that, when he said, "to restore a building is not to preserve it, to repair, or to rebuild … [but] to re-instate it in a condition of completeness which could never have existed at any given time," he meant that degrees of authenticity were under siege if architects would simply take in a case for reconstruction, maintenance, or repair. Viollet-le-Duc's argument went further to establish that a "good restoration" would have to divest its traces of contemporary conditions as a foundational requirement for a better future. But these topics were not left alone in the context of the studio.

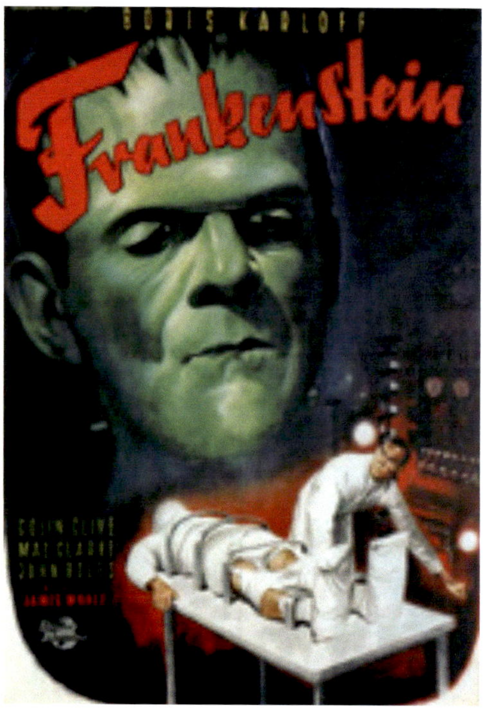

Frankenstein, The Poster (1931)

Frankenstein Movie Poster of 1931, Directed by Boris Karloff.

Soon enough, students became concerned about the dangers involved in the potential production of an adaptive reuse practice in which a monster-like object, like the one in the Boris Karloff film *Frankenstein* (1931), could be the ultimate result.

Studio participants looked carefully at the merits of the sugar mill ruins and landscapes to clarify the historic evidence, to document existing conditions, and to use such information as sparkling moments for a new future. For them, interventions in a historic environment did not necessarily require the vacuous search for a period of historic significance to which all structures should be brought back; on the contrary, in the context of the University of Miami studio, the historic environment was understood as a contemporary living medium in constant flux – a sort of supra-historic setting in which ruins were seized as unavoidable scars of a recent past in tremendous need of healing for a better future. The relationship between black and white ghosts inhabiting the space of the ruins and landscapes was celebrated with contemporary interventions in which function-specific spaces would leave traces for future rituals as well as for the comprehensive understandings of their original atmospheres and phenomenologies.

It is obvious that the existing conditions of the four colonial sugar mill host sites (Boca de Nigua, Diego Caballero, Palave, and Engombe) dictated the parameters for the student interventions. But what cannot be taken for granted is that these design proposals are a true paradigm for how to deal with difficult levels of meaning in the context of a troubled history; such conceptual tactics plus the juxtaposition of contemporary space-functions – at many scales – allowed memories of a problematic past of slavery and white supremacy to cohabit with present-day conditions in and around the historic sites.

Faculty and students assumed that the re-appropriation of difficult levels of meaning, within the context of a highly charged space, required the sensible adaptation of present-day functions into the existing spaces of the host structure without modifying its intrinsic meaning; consequently, the multiplicity of adaptive reuse programs here presented merge contemporary space-functions with the remains of the historic forms; we also understood that, new forms and new materials could not be neutral; consequently, as in the case of Gregor Samsa, adaptive reuse proposals intrinsically bring problems of content and meaning. From the point of view of culture, new meanings cannot obliterate the old, and, from the point of view of the supra-historic settings afforded by historic properties, all new functions or physical interventions, if removed in the future, should be able to retain the essential integrity of what was there in the first place.

The interventions here depicted are not justified by their power to add or subtract functional programs or economic value at the expense of the historic environments. On the contrary, they reframe the field of adaptive reuse while producing projects charged with absolute moral and ethical values and intellectual considerations; the ultimate purpose was to examine procedures and alternatives that could weave historic conditions with situations of present-day living. Moreover, the decisive drive of these projects was not to produce simple adaptive reuse interventions in their locales but to investigate their broader consequences in their surrounding contexts. Consequently, students and faculty were able to link architecture, urbanism, philosophy, culture, art, representation, and technology – the seven pillars of a true contemporary practice – into a unified block.

This was the mission of the studio, and these are its results. Judge them not for what you inherently think is right but for their power to elicit new means of understanding and new procedures for the treatment of difficult historic sites. For us, this is not the end, it is only the beginning.

INTRODUCTION

THE INGENIOS COLONIALES IN THE DOMINICAN REPUBLIC
a brief introduction

Jaime Correa and Carmen Guerrero

The Ingenios Coloniales, or Colonial Sugar Mills, are essential to the material history of the Dominican Republic. They served as a cornerstone of the national economy and as a foundation for the stability required during colonial times. From the 1500s to the end of the 1800s, sugar mills and sugar factories were founded and sustained in what is now known as "La Ruta del Azucar." The Colonial Sugar Mills not only represent a significant period in the country's history, but they currently hold significant cultural and architectural values. The students at the School of Architecture of the University of Miami explored what was left of some of the most important Ingenios Coloniales, through an innovative approach of adaptive reuse, proposed alternatives to celebrate their architectural values, cultural influences, socio-economic and racial disparities, political ideologies, and many other themes that give depth and relevance to this topic.

The Dominican Republic was discovered by Christopher Columbus during his first voyage in 1492. The island was colonized by the Spanish, who established the city of Santo Domingo, the first European settlement in the Americas, in 1496. The Spanish colonizers soon realized that the island's climate and soil were ideal for growing sugarcane, which at that moment was in high demand in Europe. As a result, they built the first sugar mills in the early 16th century; soon enough, they quickly became the main source of wealth for the Spanish colonizers. The great majority of Ingenios Coloniales were built during the 17th and 18th centuries as the most advanced sugar mills of their time. These mills were massive structures that required a significant investment of capital and labor to build and operate. The sugar mills were typically located near rivers, which were used to power their machinery, and were operated using African slave labor.

During a process of historic research, in-situ and a result of the School of Architecture Brian Canin Urban Design Gift, the students realized that, since 1492, the construction and operation of the sugar mills, particularly in the east of the island, had been carried out by Spanish colonizers who had claimed dominion of the Indian territories in the new Americas. The weather patterns in the east were essential for the designation of prime locations for the establishment of sugar mills. In turn, these small settlements of production optimally supported the growth and production of sugarcane and the enrichment of a few at the expense of an extensive slave population. The production of sugar not only provided significant economic benefits for the Spanish Empire but also allowed for the creation of an entire new social hierarchy in freshly founded cities, such as Santo Domingo.

As already stated, the Ingenios Coloniales were built and operated using slave labor, which created significant racial disparities. The African slaves who worked on the plantations were subjected to harsh conditions and were often treated as little more than property. They were forced to work long hours in the hot sun and were subjected to physical and emotional abuse. The Ingenios Coloniales also contributed to the creation of a racial caste system in the Dominican Republic. The Spanish colonizers were at the top of the social hierarchy, followed by the wealthy landowners who operated the sugar mills; the African slaves were at the bottom of the social hierarchy and had little or no social mobility.

The sugar mills in Santo Domingo were important not only for their economic value but also for their architectural values, formal importance, and site planning strategies. The Ingenios Coloniales were built in a unique style that combined Spanish and African architectural influences. The structures were typically built using a combination of local materials, including wood, stone, and brick. The sugar mills featured tall towers, known as trapiches, housing the grinding equipment used to extract juice from sugar cane. They also presented striking contrasts between the elegance and grandiosity of the house of the master and the minimalist and rather poor slave quarters. The master house buildings were often painted in bright colors and featured intricate details, such as balconies and latticework, that reflected the Spanish taste and their nostalgic approach toward Euro-centered architectures.

The Ingenios Coloniales were not just functional structures but also reflected the cultural influences of the time. The Spanish colonizers brought with them a rich architectural tradition that was evident in their design. These structures were built to withstand the harsh tropical climate, and they are excellent examples of tropical colonial architecture. The sugar mills were typically built with thick walls to insulate against the heat. The mills were also designed to be efficient, with large open spaces to accommodate the machinery needed to produce sugar. The mills' roofs were typically made of wood and were supported by massive columns, which allowed for large open spaces. These small production settlements were also designed with security in mind. They were typically surrounded by high walls, and the entrances were heavily guarded. This was necessary to protect the valuable sugar crops from theft and sabotage as well as a means to keep the slaves inside their territories.

Despite their Eurocentrism, the mills also incorporated elements of African architecture, reflecting the influence of the African slaves who were brought to the island to work on plantations nearby. The Ingenios Coloniales were also a symbol of racial disparities. The sugar mills were staffed by enslaved Africans. The Spanish colonizers used slave labor to fuel the production of sugar, and the enslaved Africans were forced to work long hours in brutal conditions. The sugar mills became a physical representation of the horrors of slavery, and the structures were a reminder of the injustice that had been inflicted on the African people; nevertheless, the sugar mills were also a site of resistance for the enslaved.

Additionally, the sugar mills were also important cultural centers. Our students learned that the mills' owners were typically wealthy landowners who were also influential in the island's politics and social life. These productive spaces were often the site of social events and religious ceremonies and, despite the horrors they were exercising over the lives of the poor slaves, the owners were expected to support the local Catholic church and sponsor cultural civic events. In spite of the brutal conditions, African slaves were able to find moments of freedom and resistance. They created their own communities, and they used music and dance as a way to express their struggle against the oppressions they faced. These cultural influences blended with the Spanish colonial culture, creating a unique fusion that is still present in the country's culture today. For our students, these sugar mills became a symbol of the resilience of the enslaved Africans, who were able to find hope and freedom even in the darkest of circumstances.

The Ingenios Coloniales also had a significant impact on the environment of the Dominican Republic. The production of sugar required vast amounts of land, and the sugar mills were built on some of the island's most fertile land. Furthermore, sugar plantations also required vast amounts of water, which were diverted from the island's rivers and streams. As a result, the sugar mills had a profound impact on the island's ecosystem, leading to deforestation, soil erosion, and water pollution.

Despite their historical significance, many of the Ingenios Coloniales in the Dominican Republic are still in a state of disrepair. These structures are vulnerable to decay, natural disasters, and neglect, and many have been lost to time. However, there are efforts underway to preserve these structures and recognize their historical significance. One of the most significant preservation efforts is the Ingenios Route (aka. Ruta del Azucar), a tourist trail that takes visitors through the historic sugar mills of the Dominican Republic. The route includes several sugar mills that have been restored and converted into museums, showcasing the history and culture of the sugar industry. These small, and very informal, museums provide visitors with a glimpse into the lives of the African slaves who worked on the plantations and the wealthy landowners who operated the sugar mills. In addition to the Ingenios Route, there are other preservation efforts underway in the Dominican Republic. The National Heritage Preservation Commission (CNPH) is responsible for preserving the country's cultural heritage, including its historic buildings and structures. The CNPH works to identify buildings and structures that need preservation and provides funding for restoration projects.

In conclusion, the Ingenios Coloniales have left a lasting legacy in the Dominican Republic. These structures represent a period of colonialism and slavery that had a profound impact on the island's history and culture. The colonial sugar mills were the primary means of producing sugar, which became one of the most valuable commodities at that time. The wealth generated by the sugar industry allowed the Spanish colonizers to maintain their control over the island and expand their influence throughout the Americas. The legacy of the Ingenios Coloniales is complex. On the one hand, these structures represent a significant achievement in colonial architecture and engineering; on the other hand, the Ingenios Coloniales also represent a period of slavery and exploitation. The African slaves who were brought to the island to work on the plantations were subjected to harsh conditions and were often treated as little more than property. The sugar mills were designed to maximize profits, and the owners had little regard for the well-being of their workers. These massive structures required a significant investment of capital and labor to build and operate. They were designed to withstand the harsh tropical climate and were often the site of social events and religious ceremonies.

In the spirit of these findings, the design work that you are about to see is the interpretative work of a group of students who took these facts seriously and whose spirit of innovation and desire for the happiness of future generations are relentlessly present throughout the pages of this small publication. Please don't be surprised by their beauty and careful execution. Their intentions were laudable, and their legacy will enlighten generations of new students to do similar work and produce urban and rural environments of prosperity and beauty.

GLOBAL PRECEDENTS

Palencia Civic Center

EXIT Architects & Eduardo Delgado

Located in the province of Palencia, Spain, this project is a remarkable example of adaptive reuse. Originally constructed at the end of the 19th century, this building served as a prison and featured brick load-bearing walls in the "neomudéjar" architectural style. The transformation of the former prison into a contemporary civic center was completed in 2011 by the architects Ángel Sevillano, José Tabuyo from EXIT Architects, and Eduardo Delgado.

The renovation process involved preserving the historic brick retaining walls while completely gutting the interior of the building. To support the addition of new floors and the roof, an independent structure was installed. Due to the poor condition of the original roof tiles, they were replaced with zinc tiles. These new roof tiles not only provide protection from the elements but also introduce skylights that allow natural light to filter into the open halls of the civic center.

The revitalized civic center revolves around a spacious central hall that serves as a unifying element, connecting the different wings. Within this central space, cylindrical courtyards made of glass were incorporated. These courtyards not only allow natural light to penetrate deep into the building but also create a connection with the surrounding natural environment.

To further enhance the functionality and aesthetics of the civic center, new pavilions were constructed between the main wings. These pavilions serve to provide additional space while contributing to a more contemporary and cohesive architectural composition.

Overall, the Palencia Civic Center stands as a testament to the successful revitalization and adaptive reuse of a historic structure. This integration of past and present creates a captivating space that celebrates both the heritage of the structure and the contemporary needs of a civic center.

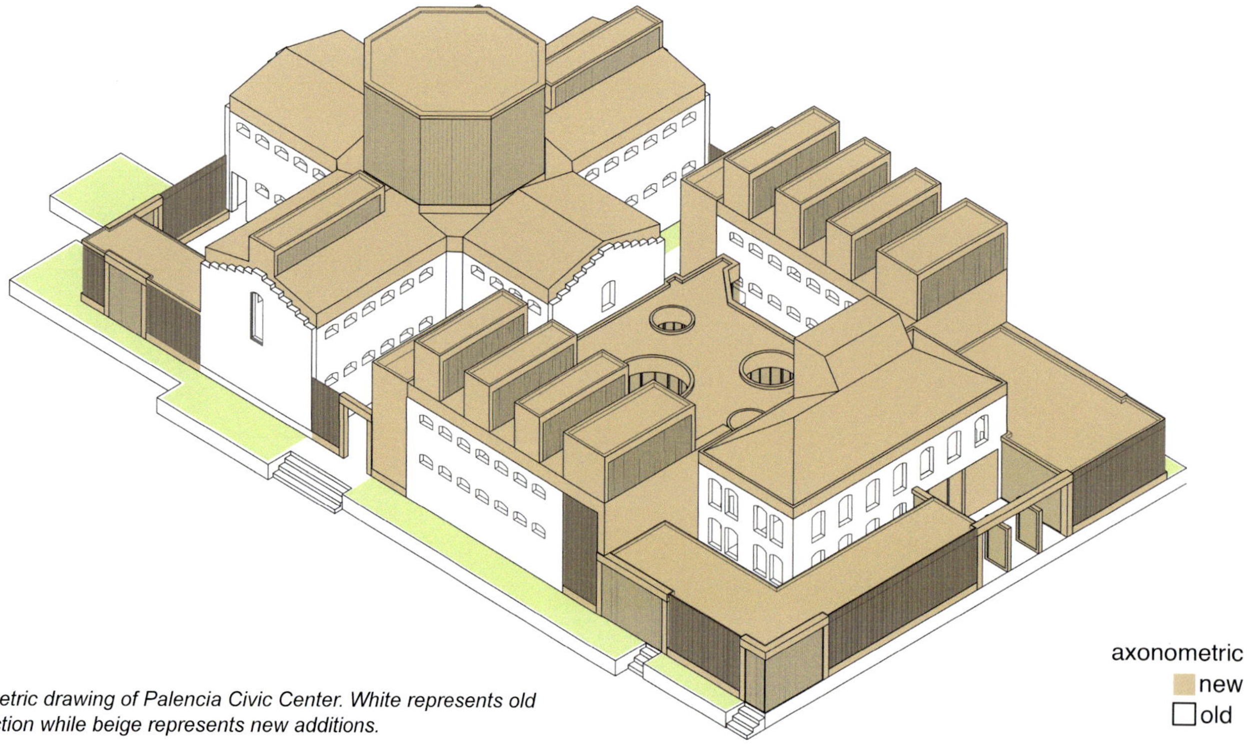

Axonometric drawing of Palencia Civic Center. White represents old construction while beige represents new additions.

Daoíz y Velarde Cultural Center

Rafael de La-Hoz

The objective of this building is to preserve the architecture of the former Daoíz y Velarde barracks by maintaining the same brick façade, basic geometry, and its saw-tooth metal structure. The actual addition happened in the interior by emptying the container of the building and creating a space for a cultural center. The space is divided in two with different entry points and circulation areas. The space is completely adaptable to many different types of events. All the spaces have a strong visual connection between each other that stimulates variations in the spatial experience.

The building offers many special innovations. The roof is high-tech and has been developed to take the best advantage of light and ventilation. The refurbishment has been made in a sustainable way regarding energy efficiency and the integration of renewable energy capture systems. It utilizes geothermal renewable energy to heat and cool the building and an air-ground exchanger that works as a mechanism for the primary renewal air. All these innovations are the reason for the final low energy cost of the building. Throughout the renovation process, the existing roof truss and its metal pillars remained suspended in the air while the interior was completed, and a new structure of concrete slabs was added to the roof. The interior lighting of the building was designed with very specific proportions regarding the structure and basic geometry of the spaces, creating a comfortable environment.

The interior wall of the old façade has the name of the heroes, Daoíz y Velarde, projected on it using yellow lights; this attribute creates a unique connection between the existing building and the addition made.The Daoíz y Velarde Cultural Center wasn't completely finished due to financial issues; the theater is currently missing seating. However, the people of the Madrid are content with the project due to the elegant manipulation of the space and the preservation of the original façade.

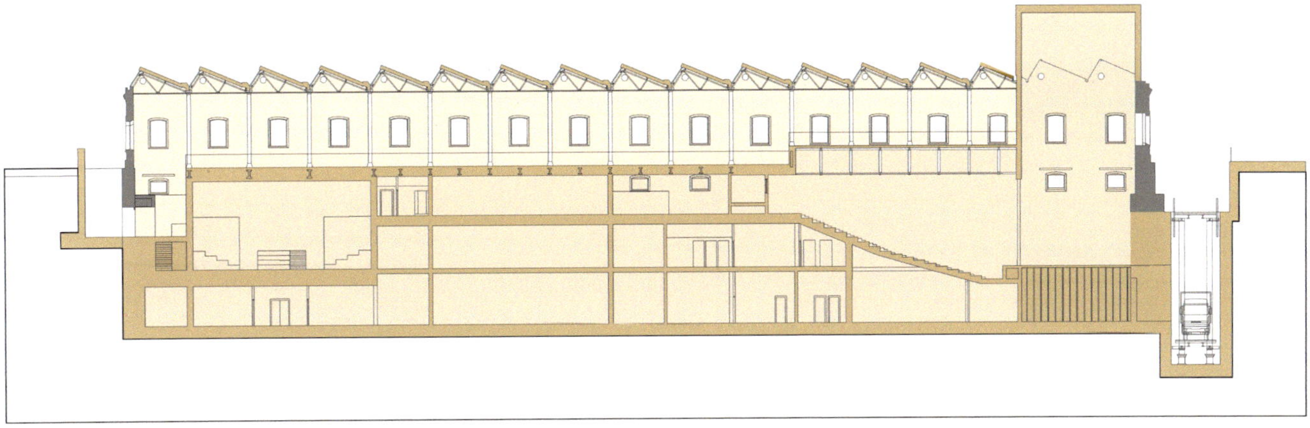

Shelter for Roman Ruins

Peter Zumthor

The Shelter for Roman Ruins is a protective shelter designed for the Roman archaeological ruins dating from 15BC. The building, located in Chur, Switzerland, was constructed mainly from timber-lamella and steel, and incorporates three individual structures. The project is located at the base of mountainous terrain. It was designed by Peter Zumthor and outlines the ruins footprint of the historic site.

The only remaining pieces of the site are the foundation and walls. Peter Zumthor's design serves as a museum and exhibition space with other Roman historic pieces. Despite having been constructed in the 1980's, the Shelter for Roman Ruins appears timelessly modern. The quality of the materiality and appearance is beyond its time. The use of timber-lamella as the exterior walls mimicks the porous material of the stone ruins.

With a modern minimalistic approach, the interior of the space only features a suspended bridge, which connects the three independent structures with one main horizontal circulation core. The lighting and the effects of the breeze become a sort of time machine; the interconnectedness between the old historic ruins and the cityscape sounds become fused with one another.

The exposed steel structure frames the space for a strong yet delicate spatial experience. Reflecting humility, warmth, and tranquility, Peter Zumthor used materiality, sound, as well as geometry to create a personal and thought-provoking space.

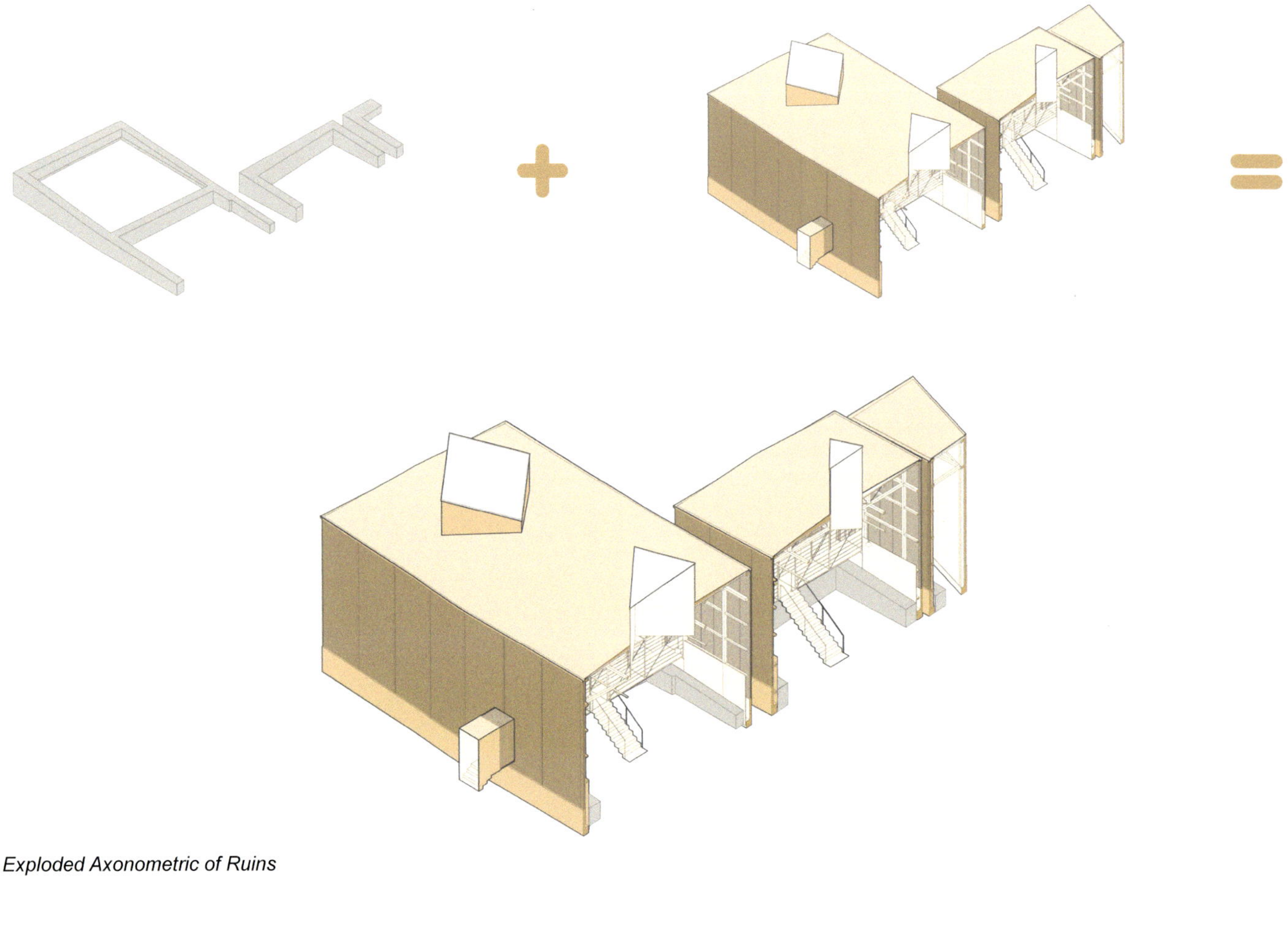

Exploded Axonometric of Ruins

Architecture Faculty

Aires Mateus

Located in Tournai Belgium, Aires Mateus, the architects of this project, take on a very powerful and meaningful site with a clear concept of merging the old and new by adapting their project design within an existing program. The Architecture Faculty occupies the interior of a historical block where existing buildings of a variety of time frames and identities coexist. Two of them are industrial buildings currently used as classrooms and a library, and what used to be a convent used as a hospital is currently proposed as an administrative program.

The new building creates a bond between the current structures by connecting them in a vertical and horizontal manner with a simple aesthetic while not coming into contact with the existing buildings. By doing so, new identity spaces are created such as passage and meeting spaces, interwined stairs, a courtyard, and an auditorium. In regards to the minimalistic white facade, Aires Mateus designed cutout windows flush with the exterior walls and excavated forms that evoke profound perpectives and views toward the historical city. This project defines new modern volume design throughout a rich site by respecting and taking advantage of what exists in a harmonious manner.

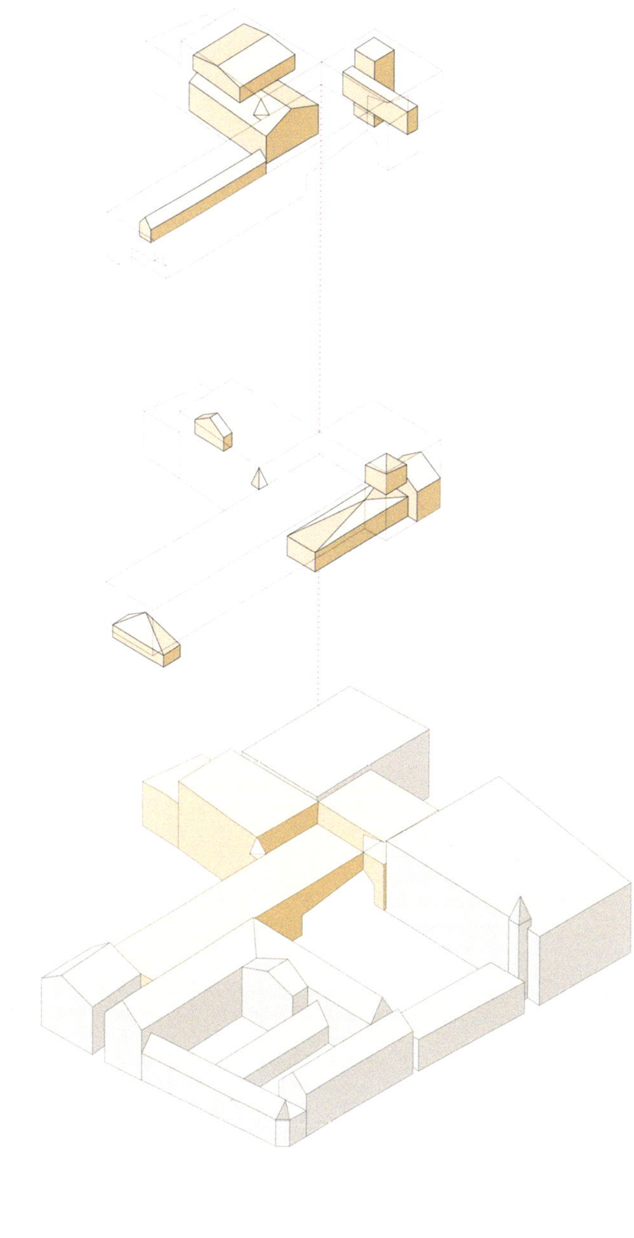

Exploded Axonometric of project

Warkteckhof

Diener and Diener

The ruins of a derelict industrial building occupied a suburban block in the outskirts of Basel, Switzerland. Between 1992 and 1996, Diener and Diener, the architects and urban designers of this project, utilized the remnants of the old building as a successful redevelopment catalyst. To complete the perimeter of the existing block, two new mixed-use buildings were added.

The first, with retail, offices, and residential uses, occupies the northernmost area of the block; the other building forms a residential courtyard with a welcoming garden – through which all apartments are accessed. The existing historic building was reused and adapted to commercial uses including restaurants, a fresh market, offices, and art studios. A corner house was kept in place and paved public spaces were provided.

The two most iconic parts of this restoration are the addition of a sculptural metallic open-air stairwell – added on the west side of the building – and a new abstract fountain with exquisite concrete details. The new set of stairs connects every floor with its free diagonal forms and provides resting places to overlook the urban landscape.

Site Plan of Project

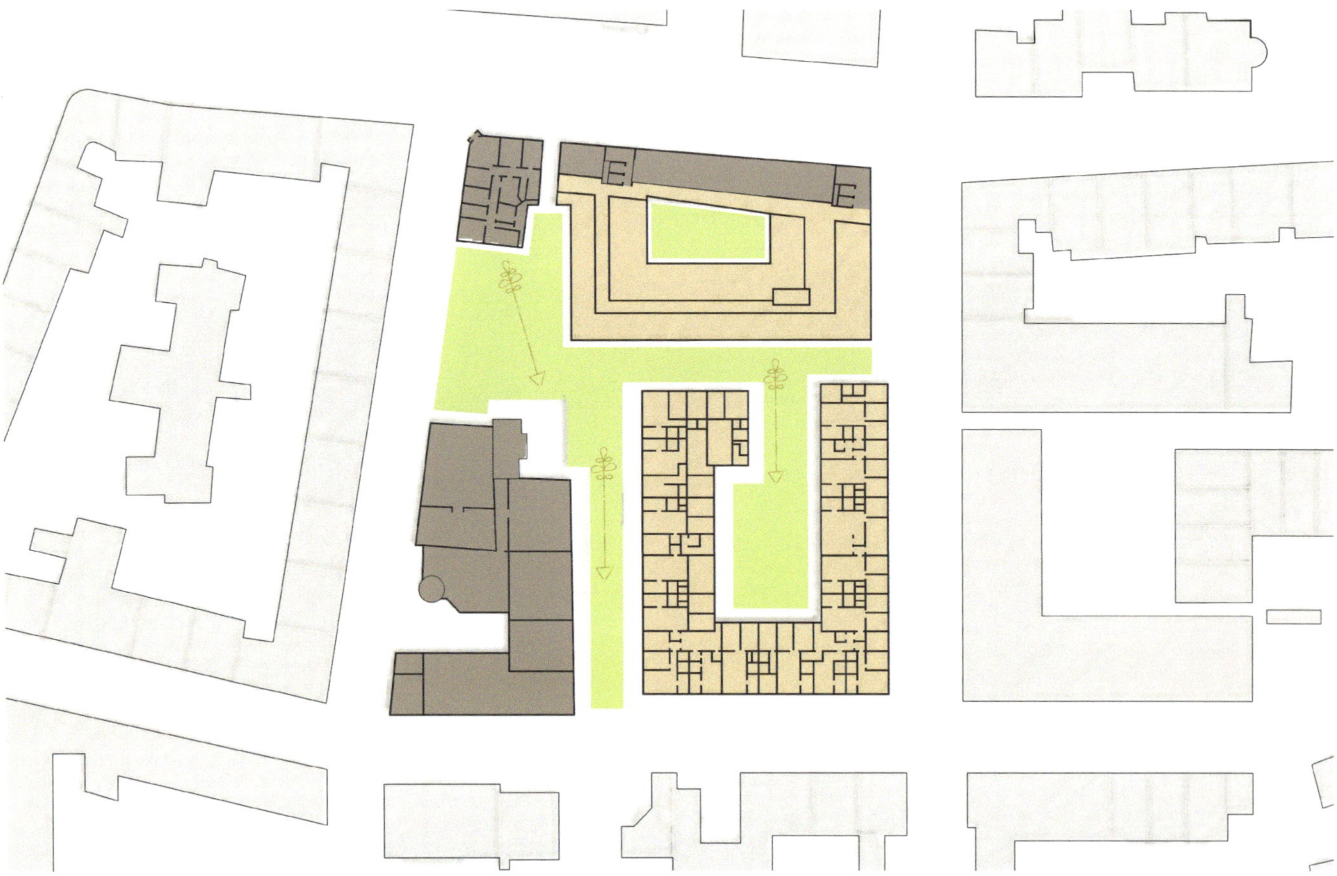

Newport Street Gallery

Caruso St. John Architects

The Newport Street Gallery was completed in 2015 for artist Damien Hirst's private collection. The building features three Victorian aged buildings sandwiched by two newly designed structures. The three center structures were built in 1913 and were used to manufacture costumes and stage sets for London theater companies. The two side buildings were added by Caruso St. John in order to create a full block of brick buildings. The interiors of the five buildings are interconnected and allow for people to move easily through the different gallery spaces.

Caruso St. John designed the interior of the gallery to be ultra-modern, contrasting with the historical façade seen from the street and adjacent rail lines. The firm had the challenge of digging out a new basement for each of the five sections of the gallery, as well as needing to add new structure to the existing historical pieces to allow for the open layout of the space they wanted. Furthermore, the use of skylights and light wells permitted the spaces to be properly lit without damaging any artwork. The award winning building has helped to both preserve the architectural history of South London, while also attracting tourists and businesses to a relatively blighted part of the city.

Front Elevation and Section

Highline Housing Project

Steven Holl

The Highline Housing Project was proposed by Steven Holl in the 1980s in Manhattan, New York. The project was supposed to be built on an old railroad in Manhattan, but was never approved; instead the railroad was turned into a park. Holl proposed that eighteen houses should be built on the old railroad, but he designed only seven. These seven unique houses are all different heights and all have different floor plans.

Holl designed seven different staircases, one for each house, including square, T-shaped, L-shaped, and spiral. Some of the staircases are indoors and some of them are outdoors. Each house also has different windows and doors; some even have light wells on top in the shape of a triangle or square. The only similarity is that each ground floor is open to allow a train to pass through if the railroad was ever reopened, or to allow pedestrians to walk freely and uninterrupted along the old railroad.

Also, all the houses have a central courtyard, and six of those courtyards have a skylight above to allow natural light. The last similarity is that each house is roughly the same length and width.

Axonometric view placed within the context of the city.

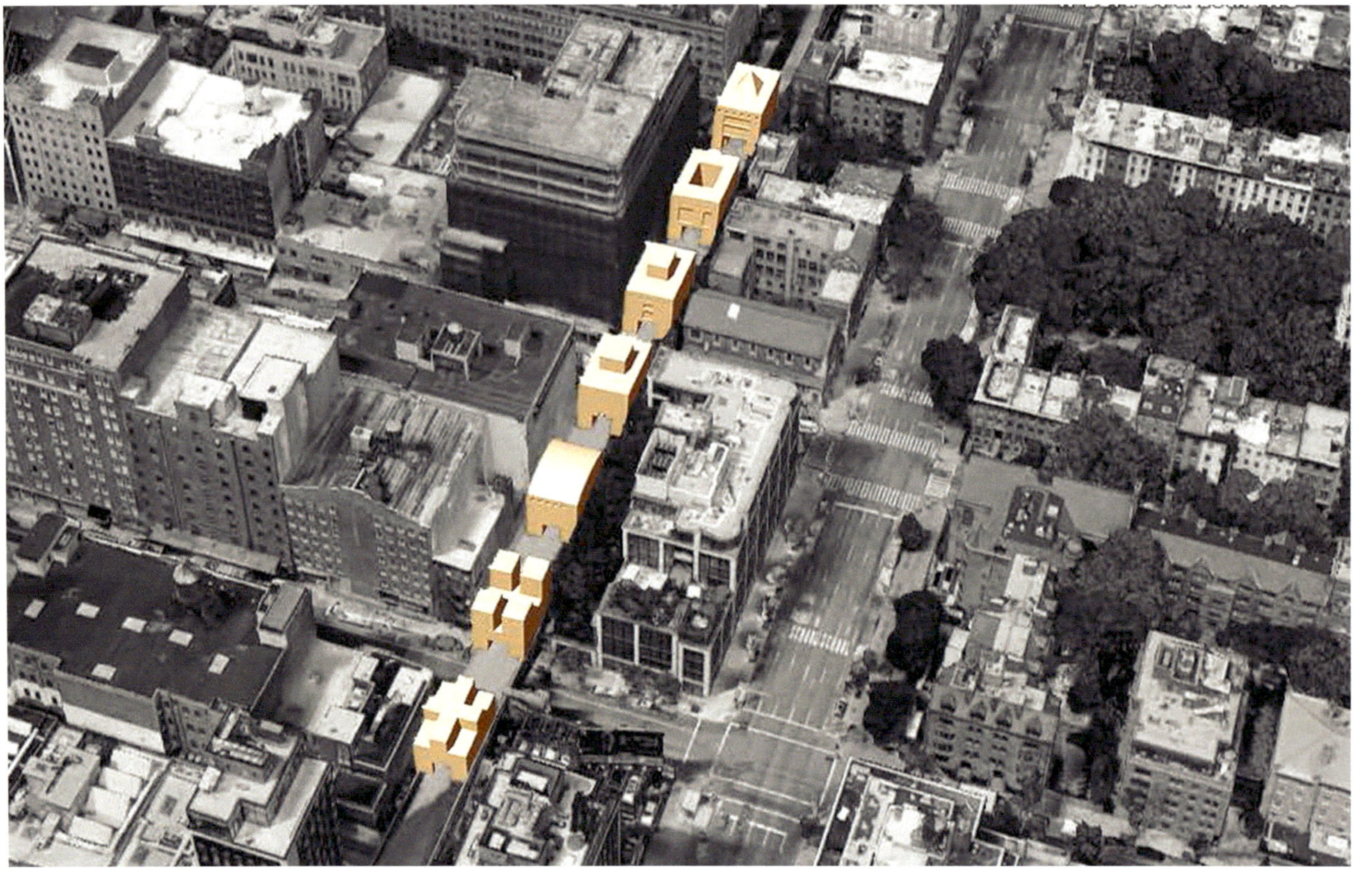

Villa Planta

Barozzi/Veiga Architects

The Villa Planta was constructed in 1876 in Chur, Switzerland by Johannes Ludwig. After its conversion into an art museum many years later, it became too small to exhibit so many artworks. In order to solve this, there was an International Architectural Design Competition in 2011 to expand the Villa Planta's exhibit space, and Estudio Barozzi/Veiga won the competition. The project was completed in 2016 but it presented itself to be very complex to the designers because the existing lot was small and it needed to have a very large program. During its design process, Barozzi and Veiga used the Villa Planta as inspiration for the new addition.

The villa was inspired by the Villa Rotonda designed by Andrea Paladio in Italy. The architects were inspired by the analysis of its components. They realized that the villa had a strong axis and geometries, giving the Villa Rotonda architectural richness, and used it in their new design.

The Kunstmuseum, as described by Barozzi, is a "NeoPaladian Building" because the decoration and ornamentation of the Villa Rotonda and the Villa Planta are transformed and used in a new way. The program of the new addition was used in a different way as well. The public spaces were placed above ground and the exhibition spaces were placed underground and connected by stairs from the Villa Planta. The underground floors are well proportioned and organized in a Paladian way. Its main material is concrete and its dimensions are 60 ft by 60 ft.

Exploded Aonometric separating old vs. new

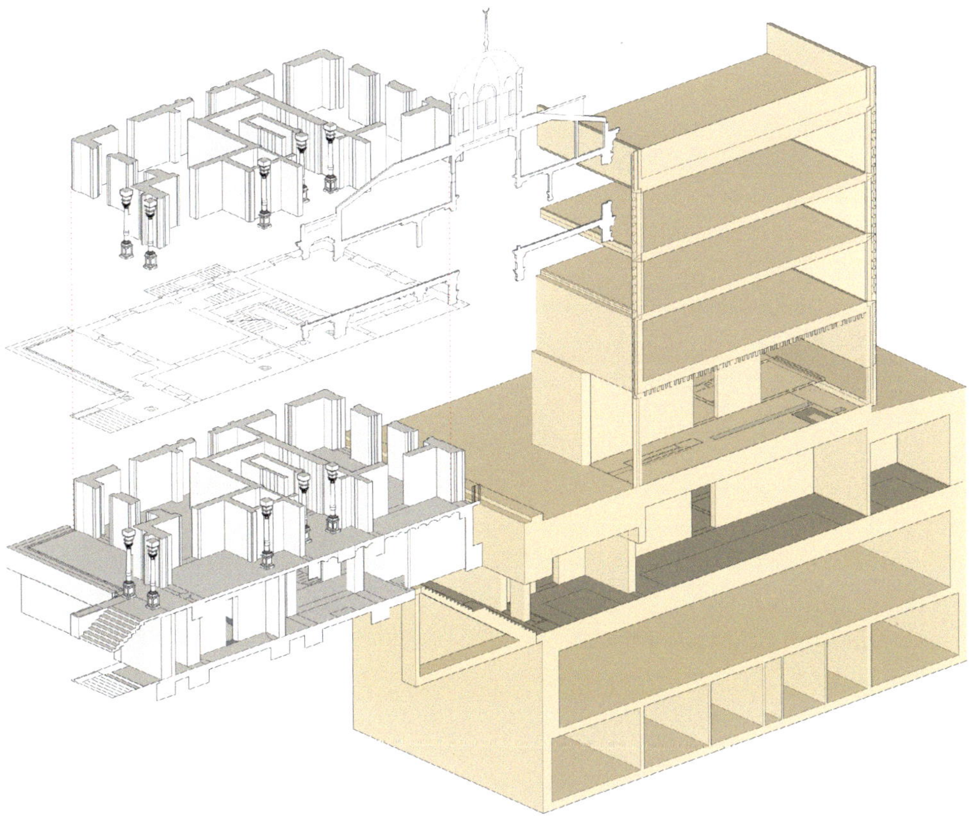

House of Twenty-Four

Fernando Tavora

House of Twenty-Four, by Fernando Tavora, is located in the medieval Town Hall of Porto, Portugal, located just a couple of yards from the cathedral. The building suffered a violent fire in 1875 which destroyed it completely and was completely redone in the year 2000. The structure was redone according to the contemporary interpretation of Tavora, who respects the formal design of the ruin and preserved the original design. The architect was able to recognize the sense of permanence and naturalness of the building and reserve it.

House of Twenty-Four characterizes a current example of the interpretation of memory in affirming the importance of a ruin. In addition, the structure is located in an isolated location, in an elevated area with the cathedral adjacent to it, accenting its importance. Tavora proves how the meaning of a ruin in architecture refers to the way a building was constructed to its primitive state.

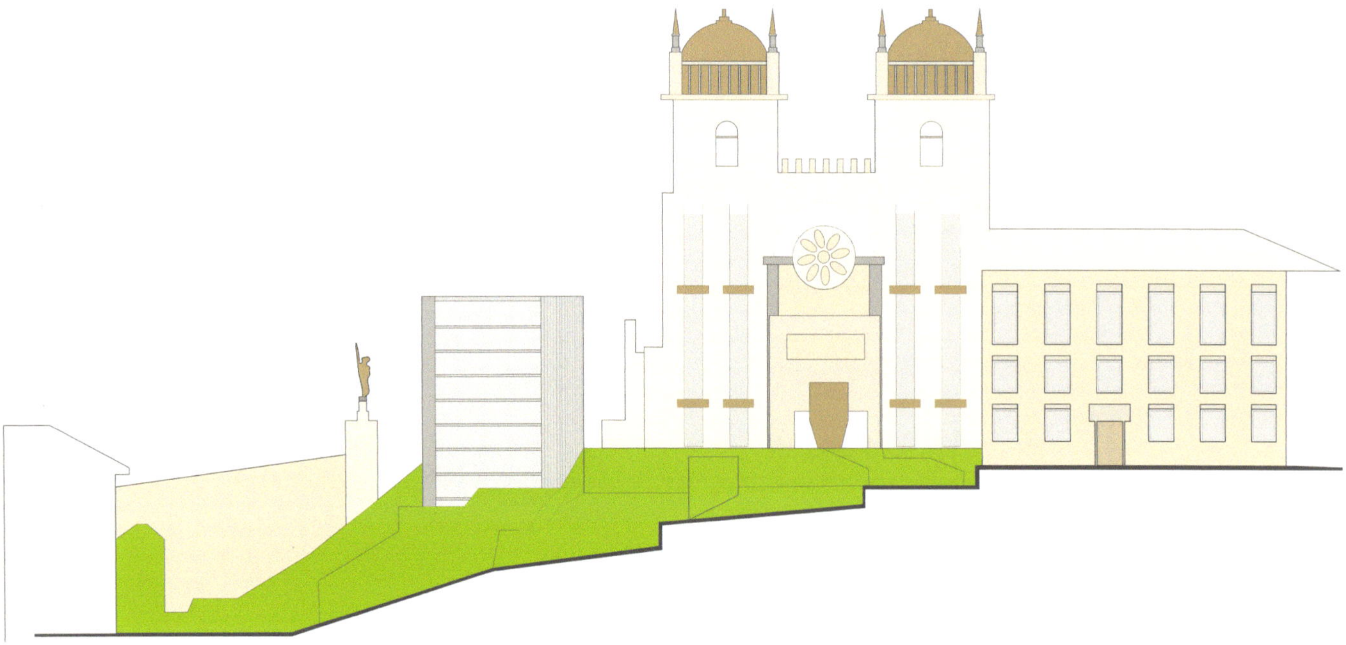

Front Elevation

Centro Cultural y Musical

Eduardo de Miguel Arbonés

El Centro Cultural y Musical was designed by Spanish architect Eduardo de Miguel Arbonés. It is located in Valencia, Spain, and was open to the public by 2004. It serves as a civic center that has an area of 2900 m^2. It has a multipurpose hall with a capacity of 400 spectators that is used as a music theater and for public events.

The only element that remains of the preexisting building is the façade that faces Plaza del Rosario. Maintenance of this element was necessary to preserve the character of the neighborhood's urban space. The façade was inspired by the classic model of the Arch of Triumph and is the only entrance into the building. It is bounded by party walls and therefore it is almost impossible to establish a direct relationship with the outside.

That being said, the design was inspired by the existing site conditions and the surrounding buildings. The most noticeable feature of the project is the double wall that contains circulation and allows natural light through. There are various skylights strategically located throughout the project that bring delicate paths of sunlight into the interior.

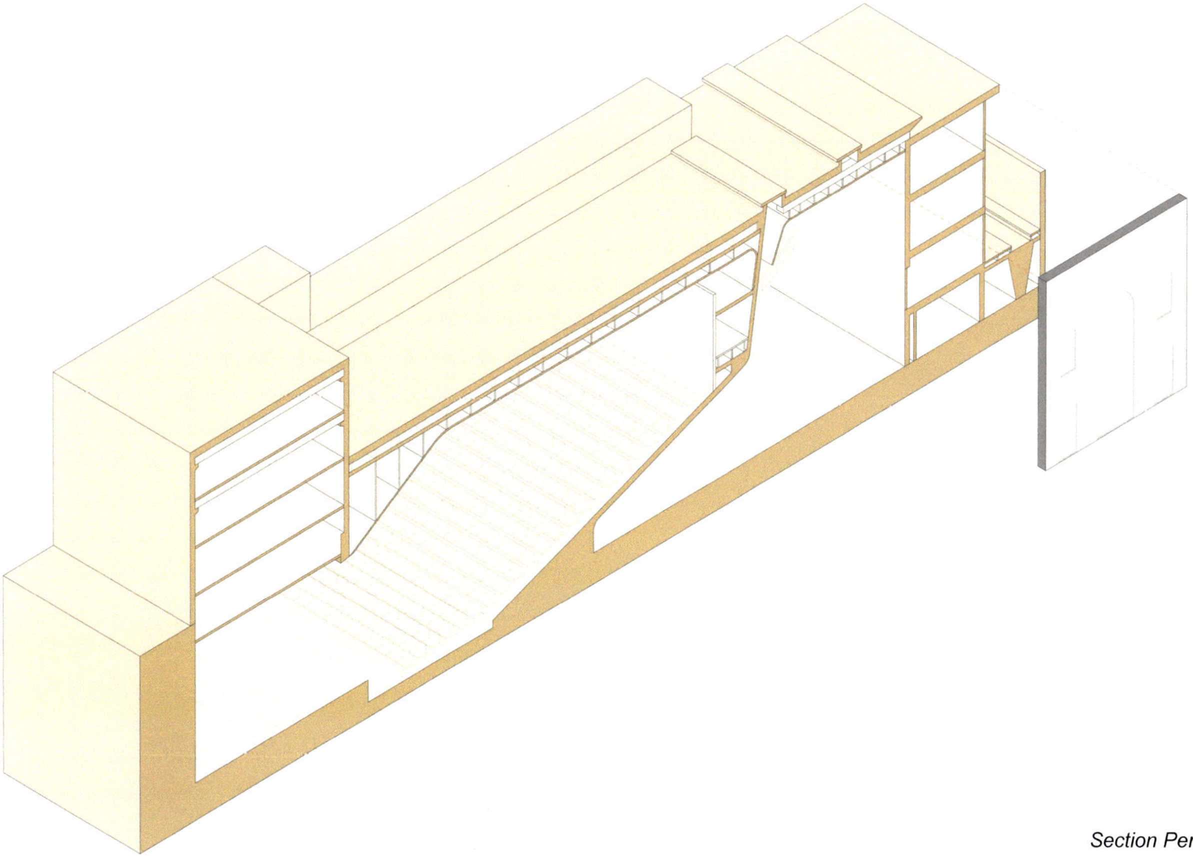

Section Perspective

Museum of Contemporary Art of Rome

Odile Decq and Benoit Cornette

The Museum of Contemporary Art of Rome (MACRO) was designed by Odile Decq and Benoit Cornette in 2001, and it was built from 2002 to 2010 in Rome, Italy. It was added to an existing building that was built in 1912. The architect wanted to keep the majority of the building, so she integrated the whole block into the new building.

One of the interesting concepts of the design is how Odile wanted to integrate the contemporary art and the structures together. As a result, she designed the exterior and the interior structures of the new building to have a dynamic concept to give the visitors a different urban experience. The building is made out of steel and glass which will help let the light pass through the ceiling and into the interior garden. The museum consists of exhibition halls, auditorium, coffee shop, restaurant, bookstore, meeting rooms, and an aboveground parking.

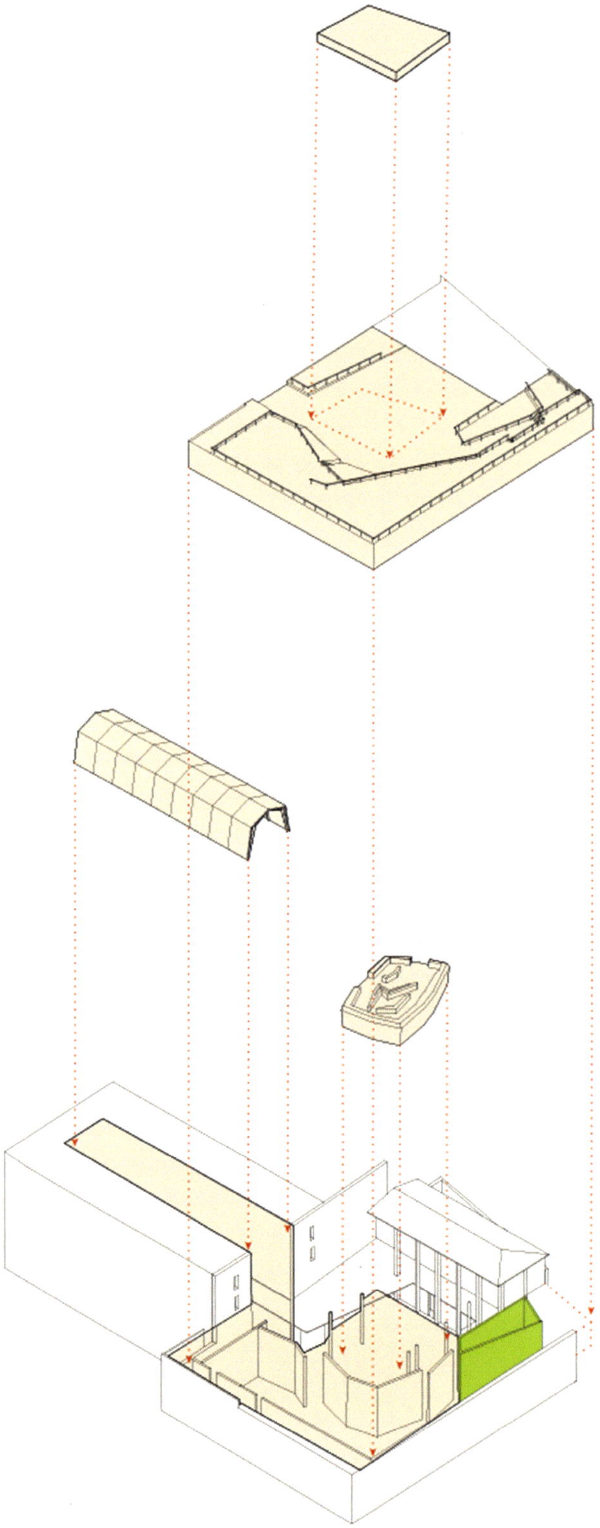

Exploded Axonometric

Sagunto Roman Theater Center

Giorgio Grassi and Manuel Portaceli

The Teatro Romano de Sagunto is a Roman theater, in Sagunto, Spain, located in Valencia. They declared the ruins Bien de Interés Cultural in 1896. The Roman Theater of Sagunto is located at the foot of the mountain crowned by Sagunto Castle. After being declared Bien de Interés they decided to preserve what was still there. This project inhabits the transitional terrace, between the city and the upper platform that is being managed by the Forum, and it has become the Civic Center of the city, re-joining to an urban planning from the times of Emperor Augustus.

The architect who was granted the project of preserving this building was Giorgio Grassi in 1935 with the help of Manuel Portaceli, later in 1942.
It is believed to have been built back in the middle of the first century by using the slope of the mountain. The project itself is composed of two major parts, the first being the cavea or grandstands, a semicircular shaped seating arrangement for spectators and composed of three orders of stands and the stage, this piece has the capacity to seat 8,000 people. Amazing the way the architect protects and interprets what could have been there before. By adding a roof to the building, it is safe to say that the idea of keeping the project an open space would help to preserve the project while exposing most of its materials.

Section of Project

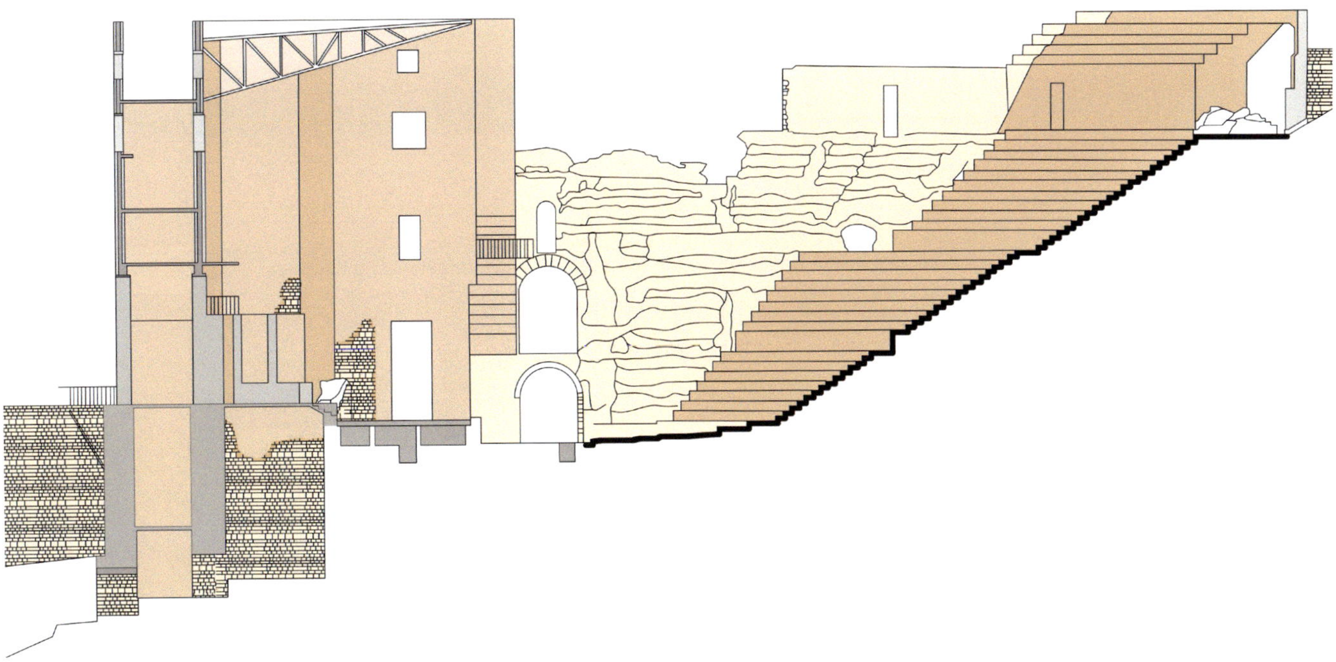

Slaughterhouse Renovation

Gonzalez and De la Cruz Architects

Medina is a historic town renowned for its whitewashed walls and ceramic roof tiles. The architects for the villa had the opportunity to renovate the 19th century slaughterhouse into a cooking school. They analyzed the location and considered the topography in Medina.

The small town lies in a valley, which influenced the design. Gonzalez and De la Cruz decided to approach the renovation by "settling in its empty spaces"; they created pitched roofs that lay on top of the existing whitewashed perimeter wall.

The pitched roofs were supposed to imitate the intense topography of Medina. However, they were also intended to capture natural sunlight that properties like these lacked; in turn they inserted several light wells with small gardens between the pitched roofs.

The ceramic roofs make an impactful statement in Medina, the city considered by many the oldest in Europe. Gonzalez and De la Cruz's approach to the renovation is beautiful because it is subtle; the changes they made are adaptations of concepts that make up the old city.

Exploded Axonometric

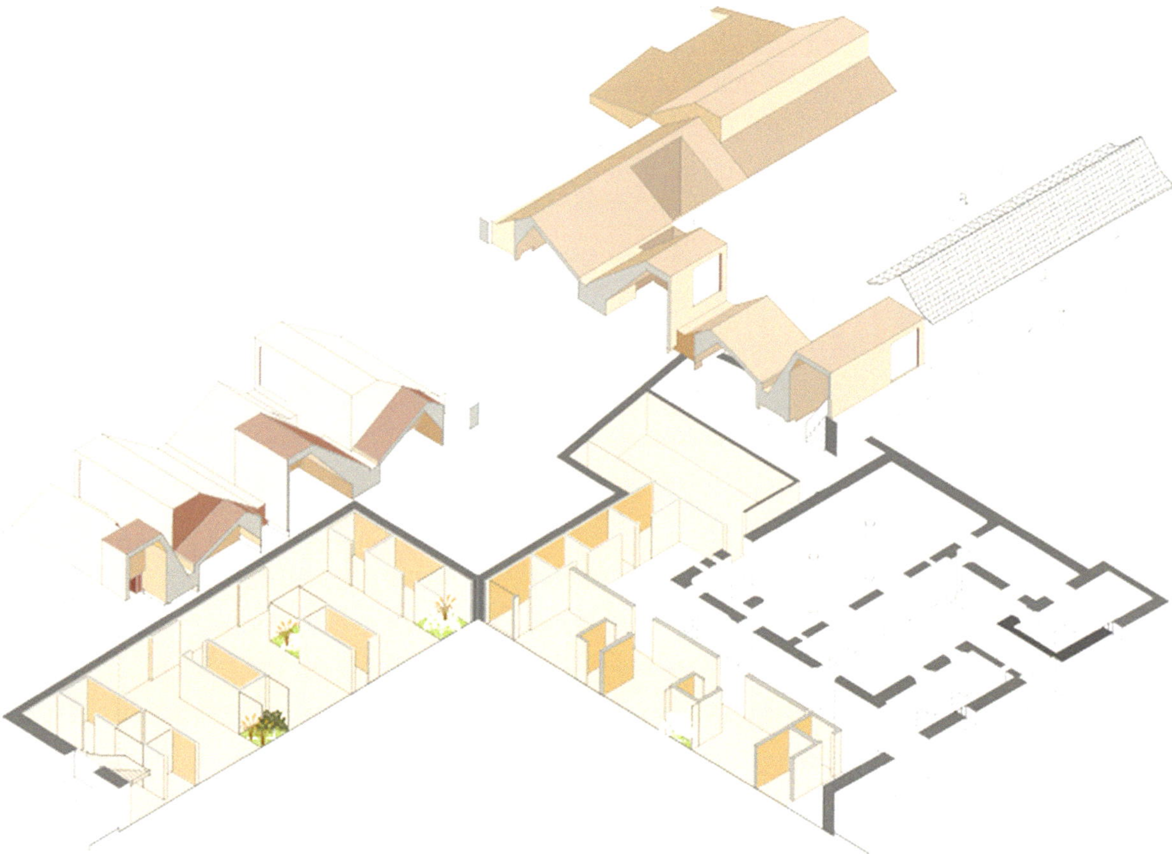

Centro Cultural y Musical

Rafael Moneo

The project is taken from a competition to restore and preserve the San Francisco Ruins in the colonial city of Santo Domingo located in the Dominican Republic. The winning project, from Spanish architect Rafael Moneo, was the perfect combination of preservation, modern architecture and urban development. In his proposal he, not only created a new structure for the Monastery, he also created a whole new concept for the surroundings of the site.

He proposed a reconstruction of historic walls, a new bridge, and numerous public parking areas thoughtfully placed to take you to the historic sites, parks, and plazas. In terms of the main building, he created a modern white structure to intervene in the church and a new annex to merge into the left side of the church.

He first proposed a new cover for the structure maintaining its original base that is still left in ruins. He then proposed a theater or auditorium in a more modern style right next to the church. Finally, he added the event center with a communal green space.

The way in which the restoration is conceived is what makes the project so successful; he has made it possible to perceive the volumes and the spaces of the old monastery. It brings some modern features like open air corridors, screen facades, and big windows but still takes you back to what was existing at some point.

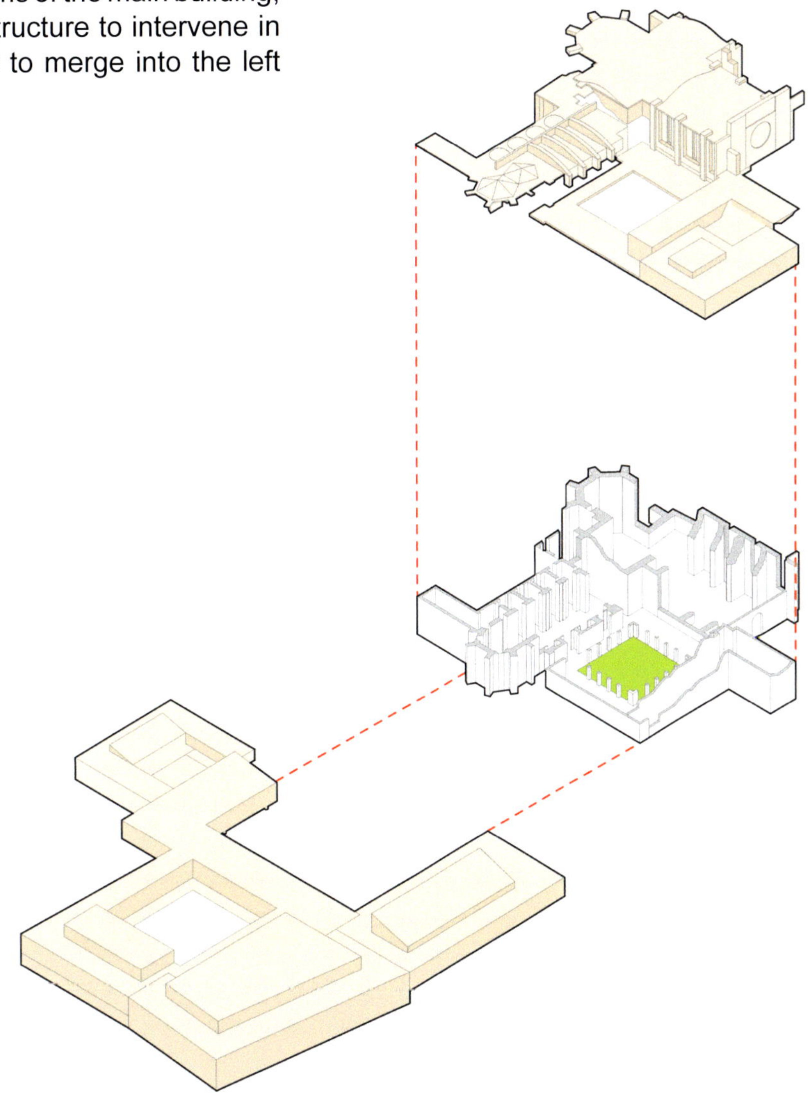

Exploded Axonometric

Kolumba Museum

Peter Zumthor

A late Gothic church, one of many incarnations built upon Roman ruins, was bombed in World War II, reduced to a few standing fragments and rubble. The site lay vacant for decades, exposed to the elements, until the Archdiocese of Cologne commissioned Zumthor to build a museum atop the ruins to house his collection of religious art and relics in 1997.

Zumthor executed an unusual design, built literally atop the stone wall fragments, with new, Roman-style bricks nestled right into the historic fabric, creating a delicate envelope that covers the ruins while leaving them on display.

His preservation strategy is novel, both daring and sensitive, and I think brilliant. He leaves what was once the main sanctuary open, with a series of delicate columns and a meandering walkway the only interventions in a pool of rubble, designing a careful set of experiences indoors and out, through the ancient and the modern.

The galleries exist above this volume and to the side in a modern addition. In lieu of many windows, Zumthor lays the bricks with spaces in between, acting as a screen to delicately filter light, leaving the volume pure and only puncturing it in strategic transition points between spaces.

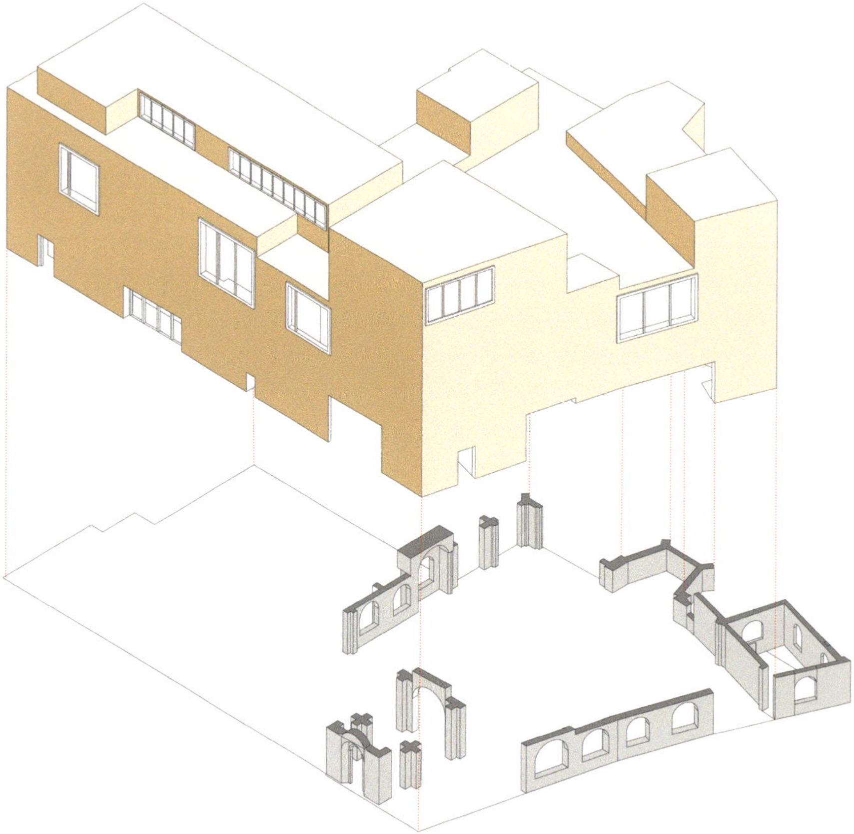

Exploded Axonometric

University Hospital

H. Baur, E. + P. Vischer, and Bräuning Leu Düring

Clinic 1 was originally built in 1945 and viewed as an example of modernisim in Basel, Switzerland. Designed by H. Baur, E. + P. Vischer, and Bräuning Leu Düring, the modern classic maintained functional organization and high architectural quality. In 2003, a new surgery unit and maternity wing were added, but were still integrated to complement the original 1940s Swiss clinic. The intervention adopts the same architectural order of stories, proportions, courtyard typology, and load-bearing structure.

Thus, the additional Women's Clinic continues the existing building form to maintain harmony while still acting as its own entity. To offer column-free interiors, vertical technical shafts line the interior atrium, and the outermost columns are arranged on a grid. The double façade and fully glazed elevation filters light while providing privacy and protection from glare.

Natural light is made present in all circulation and communal spaces due to the lighting from the façade and the central atrium. Five triangular ramps fronting the façade were formed in the ground to provide light to underground laboratories.

The concentric square structure offers flexible use of space and the extension was constructed with in-situ concrete elements/cement.

Exploded Axoometric

PROJECT LOCATIONS

Sosua
Puerto Plata
Cabrera
Rio San Juan
Nagua
Las Terrenas
Samana
DOMINICAN REPUBLIC
Hato Mayor
San Pedro de Mac
INGENIO PALAVE
Santo Domingo
Boca Chica
INGENIO
San Jose de Ocoa
INGENIO DIEGO CABALLERO
San Cristobal
INGENIO BOCA DE NIGUA
Azua
Bani
INGENIO DE SAN GREGORIO
Vicente Noble
INGENIO DE CEPI
Barahona

Lagunas de Nisibón
Punta Cana
Higuey
Dominicus

PROJECTS

Ingenio Boca de Nigua

The history of the Ingenio Boca de Nigua includes stories of slavery, emancipation, liberation, and the production of meaningful architectural artifacts. The building composition is the result of many small architectural iterations which, in proper time, became objects with an astonishing legibility, extraordinary congruency, and functional simplicity. The Ingenio Boca de Nigua goes back to the sixteenth century and, as such, it is among the first sugar mill factories in the French Caribbean.

It is located near the small town of San Gregorio and west of the Nigua River; its humid climate, in conjunction with the heat required for sugar production, turned this sugar factory into one of the most undesirable places for slaves in the Dominican Republic. During our visit to the site, the local historian recorded that "young slaves were bought as disposable commodities"; he basically meant that "the owners were well aware that no human would be able to work in these hellish facilities and survive more than eight years."

The existing complex consists of the ruins of a "Casa de Calderas" with 12 sugar boilers (50% restored between 1974 and 1978 by Ramon Baez Lopez-Penha), the "Trapiche," a polygonal building where the sugarcane was squeezed with the help of oxen, the residence of the slave master or "Casa Principal" of which only the foundation can be seen, a small tower for drying and storage, and a series of underground caves for the refrigeration of raw sugarcane juice, or "guarapo." The main residential courtyard was later used for other purposes, including ovens for ceramic production, and vestiges of its later uses can be identified as ruins on the land surface. In 2005, Ingenio Boca de Nigua became a UNESCO Monument for the Patrimony of Humanity.

Ingenio Boca de Nigua

Daniella Cancel & Daniella Huen

Named Hotel Ana María after the slave who led the first rebellion in the New World, this hotel is centered on the history and culture of this important Dominican site. The materiality of the building honors the multiplicity of layers of construction occurring through the years.

The first layer is the original construction, which this proposal leaves untouched; the second is the historical reconstruction of the 1970s, left untouched; and the third layer is the proposal itself – which follows the same foundation footprint lines of the original construction but assumes an interpretative role with a new kind of materiality as a means to distinguish the time differences.

The project uses include an entrance lobby, a gift shop, a pool, a spa with several smaller pools for a diversity of treatments, a restaurant, a museum – under the space of the restaurant and where visitors can experience the dark history of the site – and the hotel proper. The proposal also includes courtyards and gardens that can be used for outdoor activities.

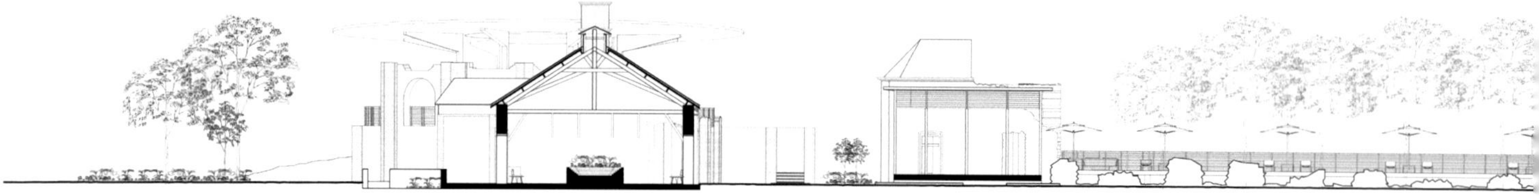

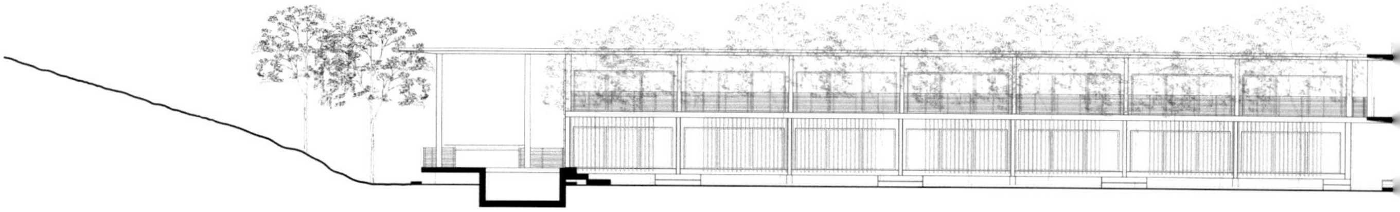

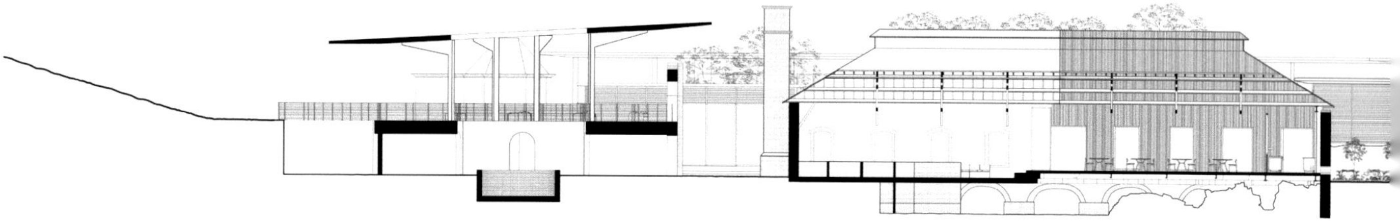

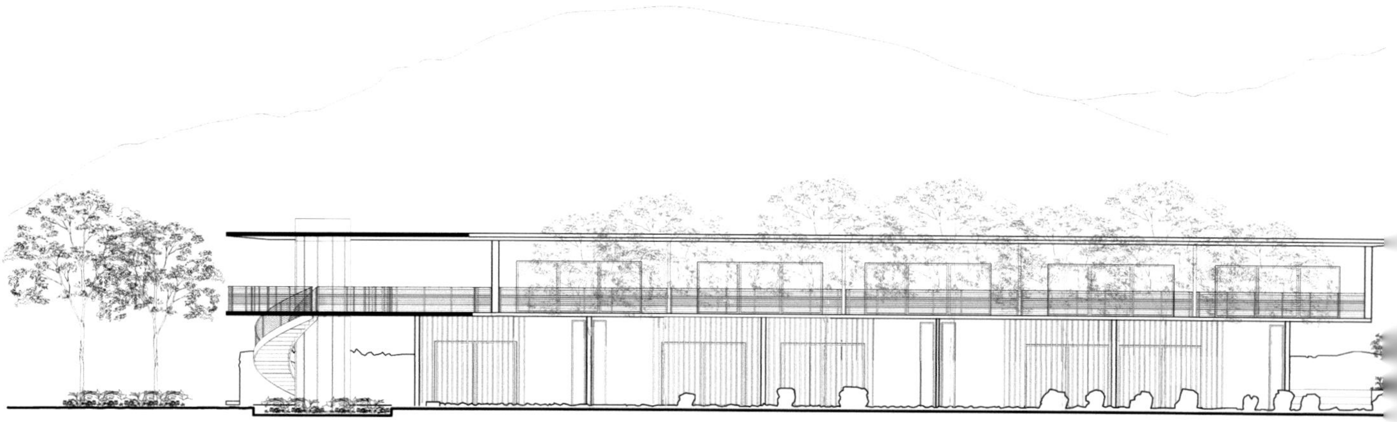

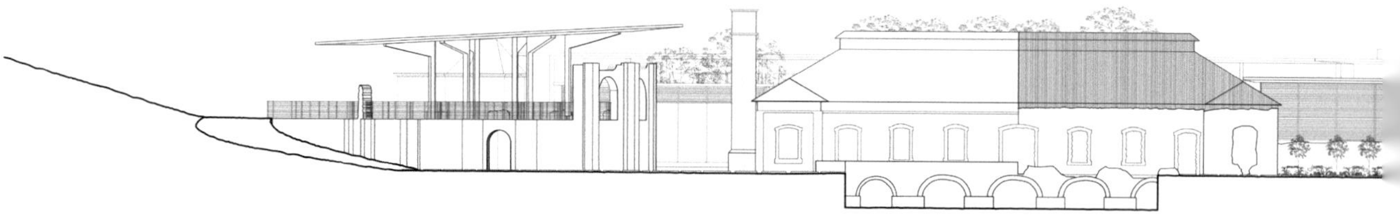

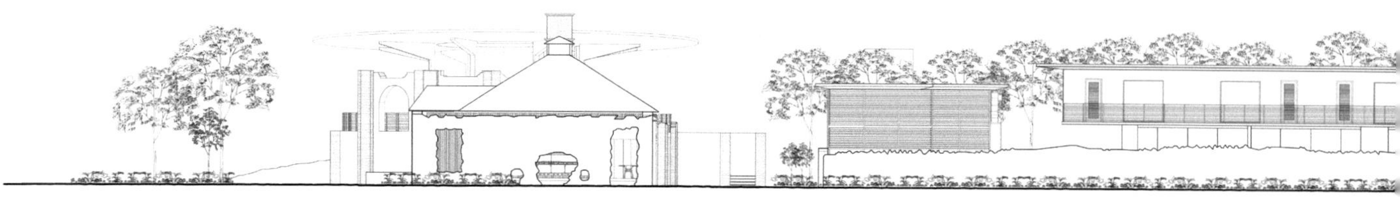

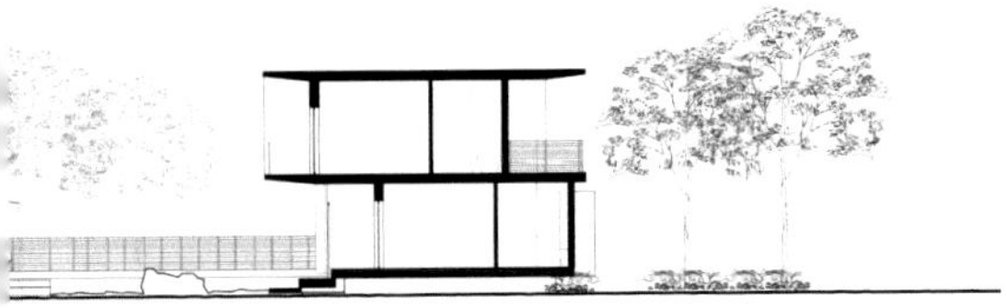

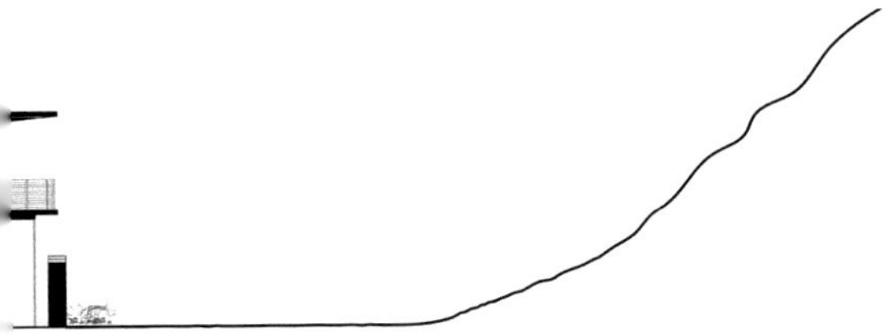

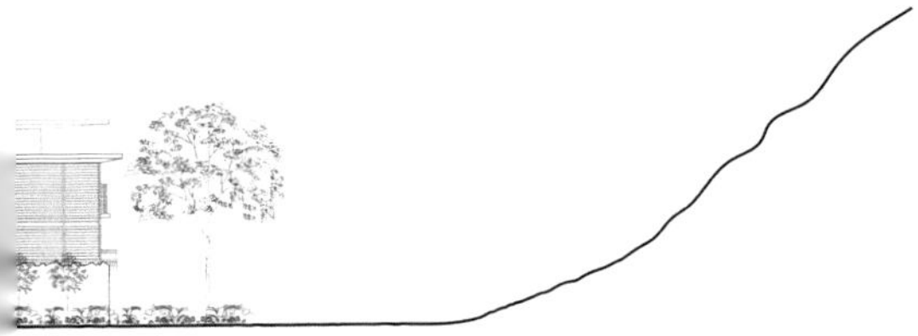

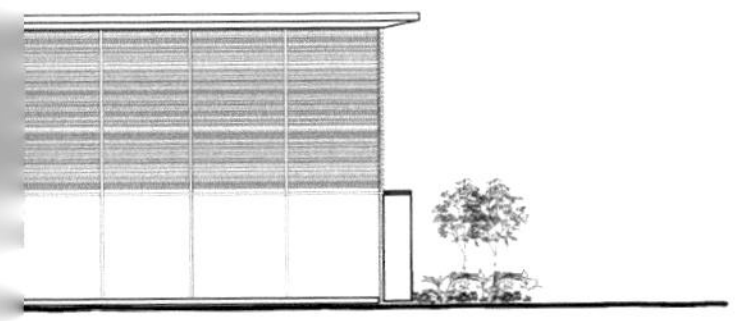

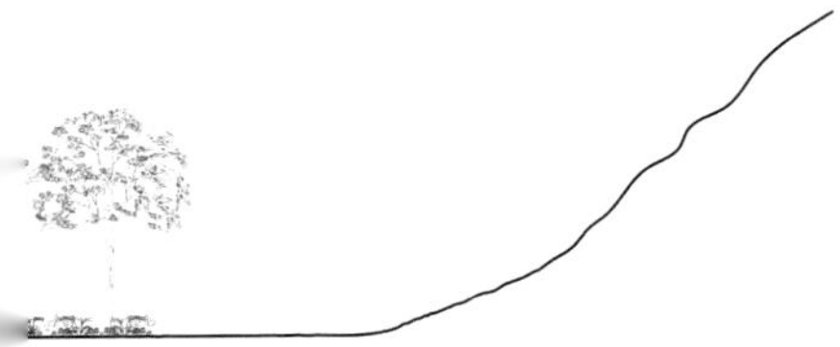

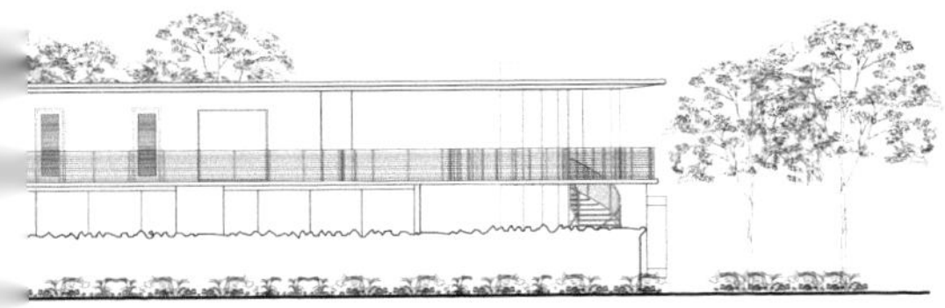

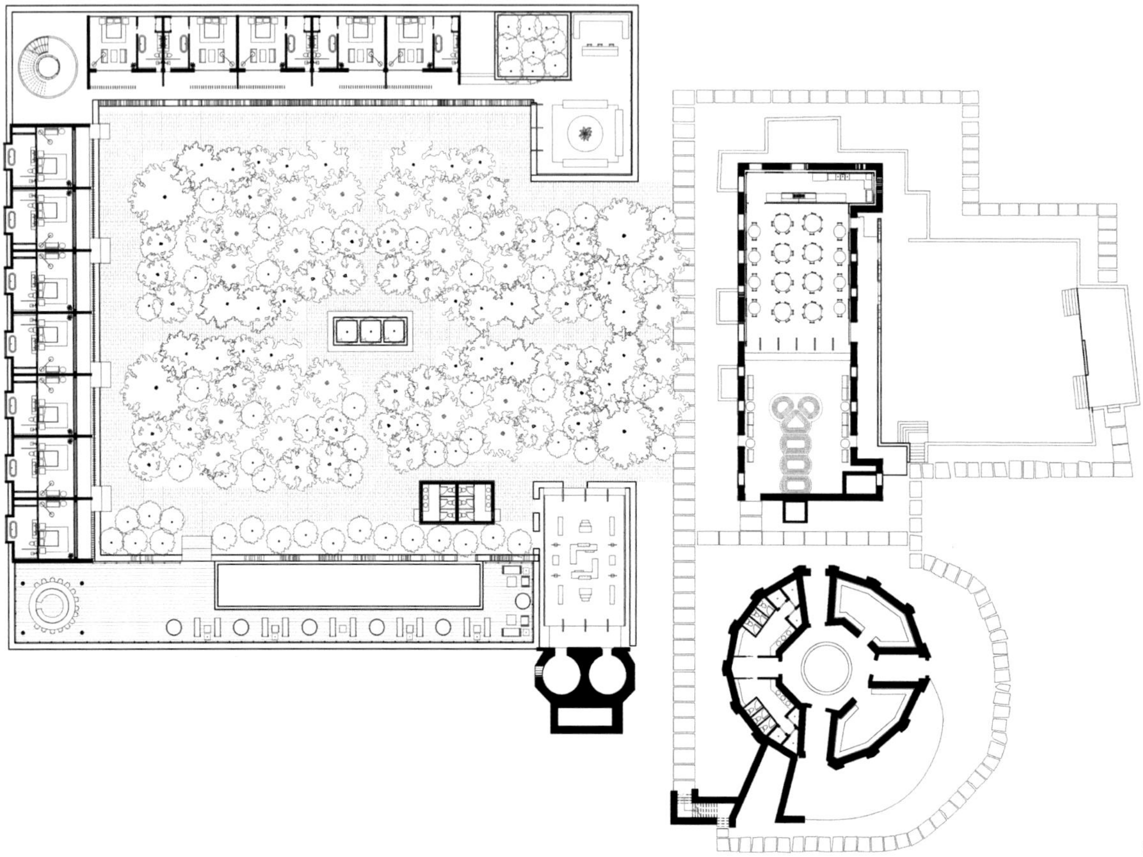

Ground Floor Plan

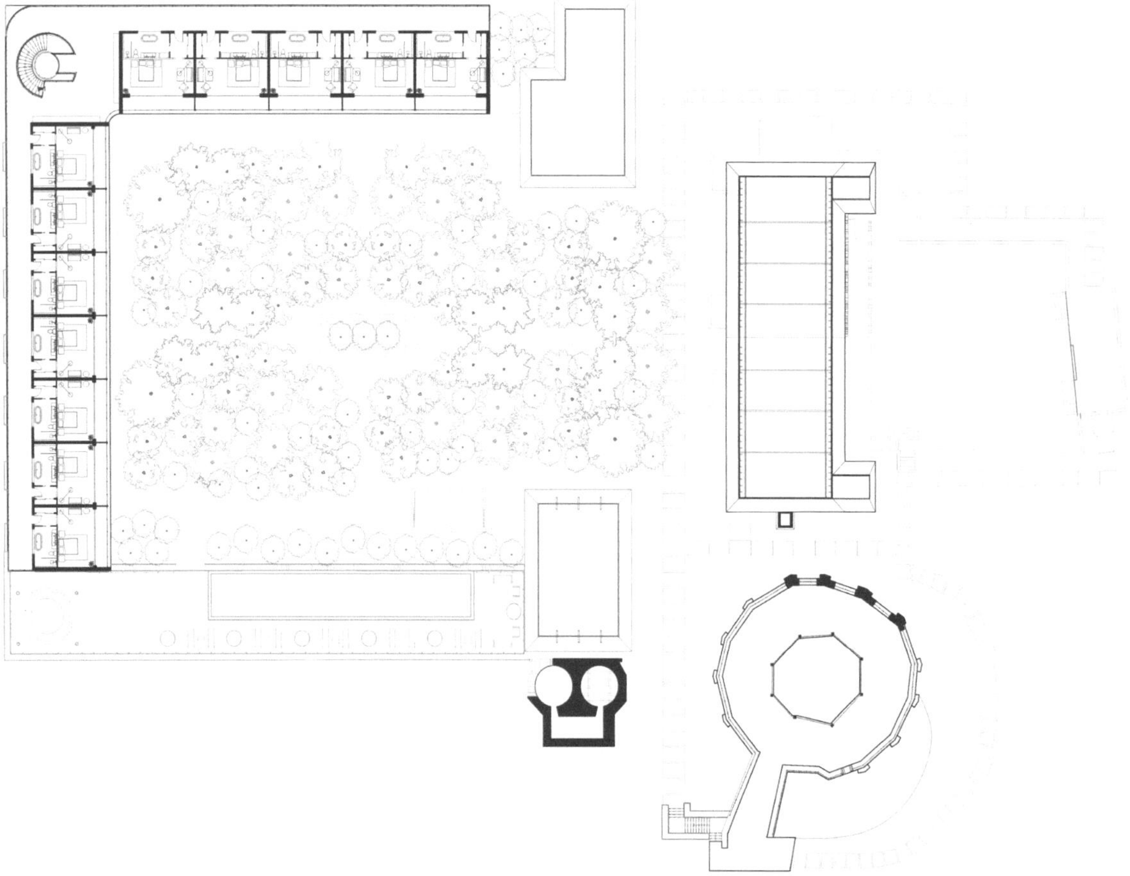

Second Floor Plan

Current page, interior view of restaurant located in the original Casa de Calderas. *Facing page, top,* Ground Floor Plan, *bottom,* Second Floor Plan

View from courtyard to lobby

Above, view of hotel rooms. *Bottom left,* view toward redesigned trapiche; *bottom right,* interior view of gift shop

Hotel spiral stairs

Hotel window detail

Interior view of hotel room

Aerial view of project

Ingenio Boca de Nigua

Catalina Chaves & Adrianna Rivera

As a conglomerate of educational, relaxation, and commemorative uses, Las Ruinas presents a new beacon of contemplation for the community of San Cristobal. Keeping the needs of the community in mind, while acknowledging and materializing the history and significance of Boca de Nigua, this proposal re-imagines how such a historic site, with its unfortunate and morally questionable past, may be able to transform itself into a real place for the cultivation of a future with a positive human impact.

Once used by some of the first New World industrialists for sugarcane production, Las Ruinas preserves, rehabilitates, and reconstitutes existing and historic structures as well as the historic traces still legible on the ground. The proposal establishes a great preservation feast as well as a place of remembrance of the dark history of African American slavery in Santo Domingo.

The intervention incorporates land uses which commemorate the past, acknowledge the present, and edify a better future. Las Ruinas incorporates an Academia, specialized in the studies of Caribbean Architecture on the foundational traces of buildings which do not exist anymore. This new building provides

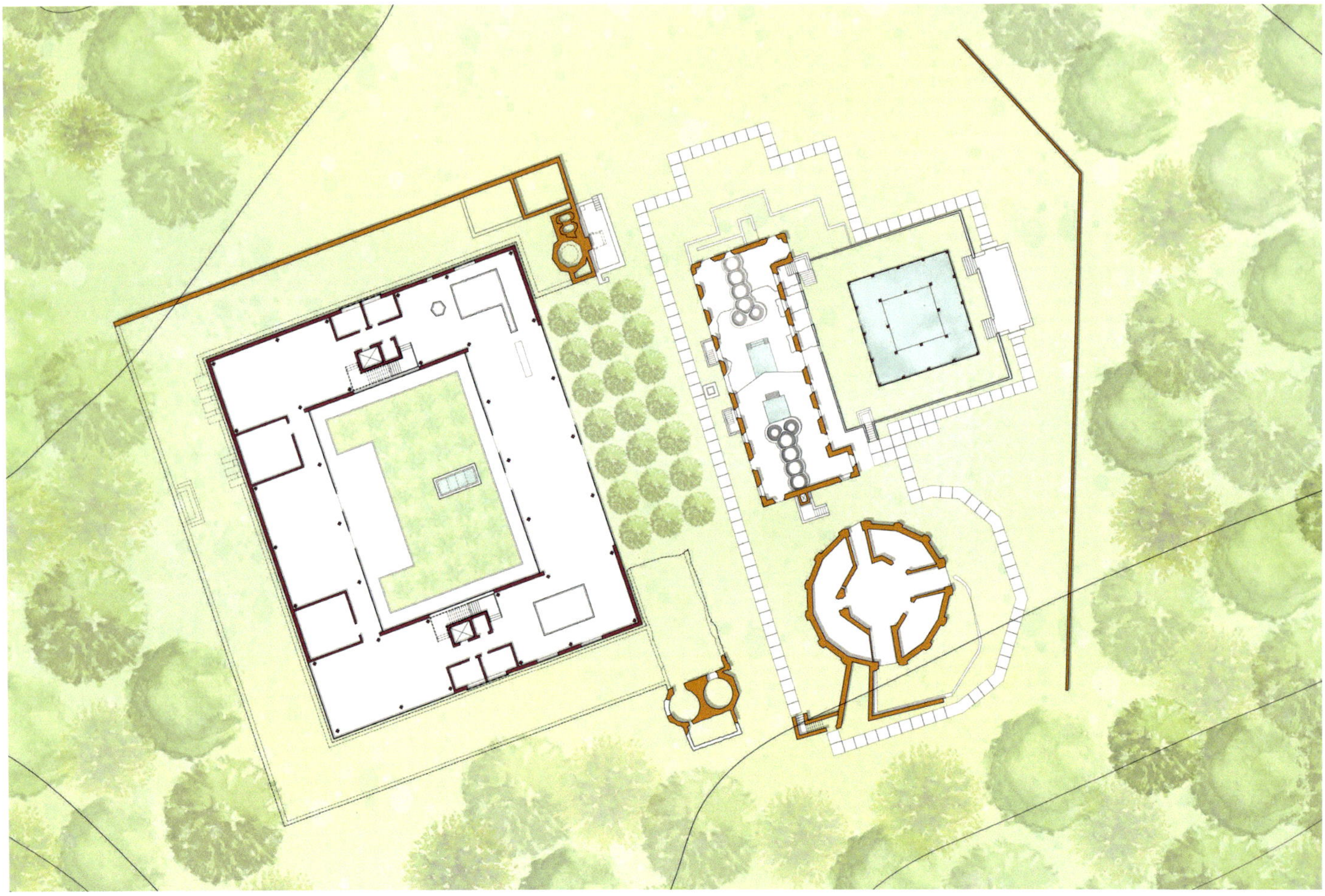

First floor

Façade View

Façade View

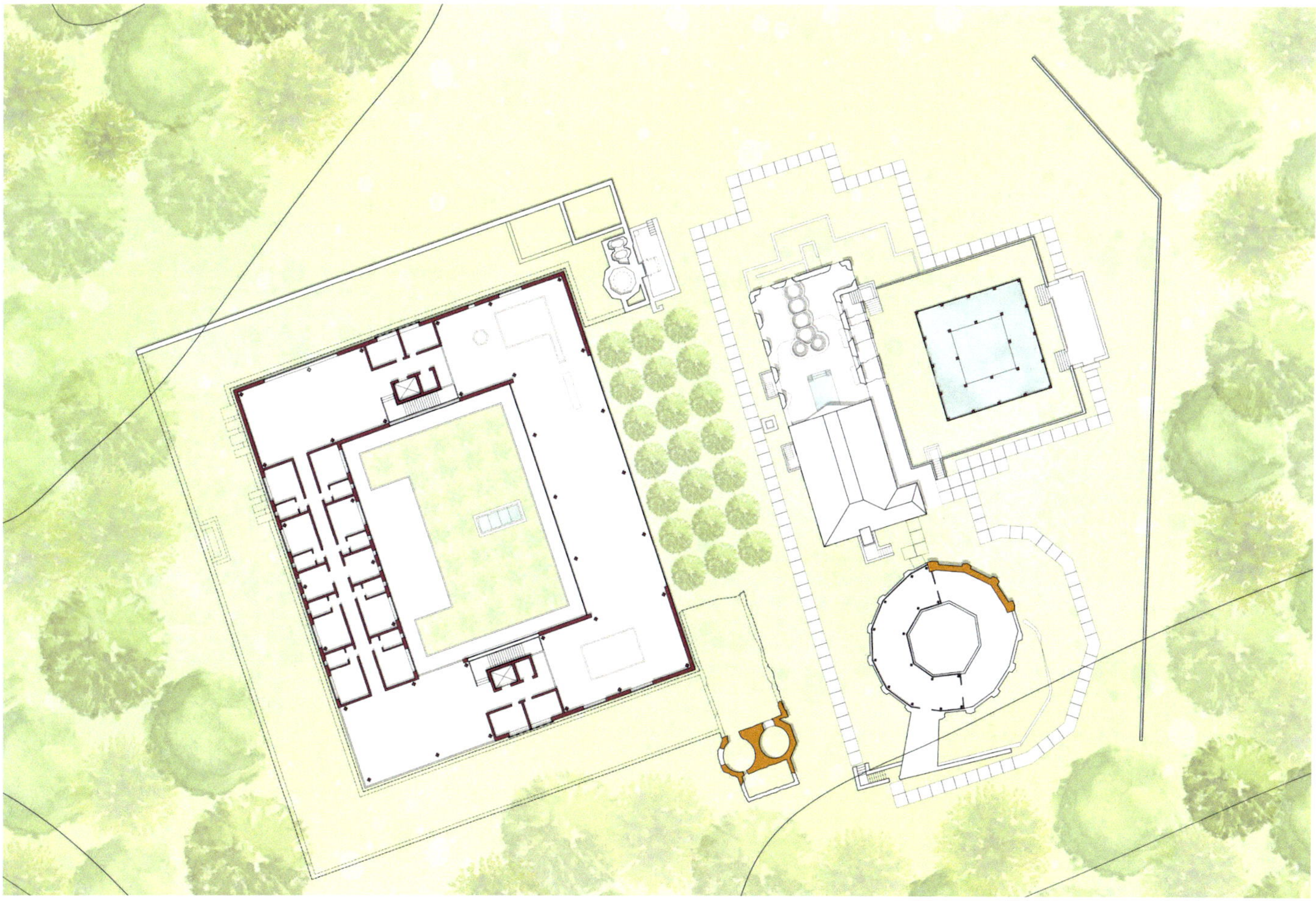

Second Floor

Building Section

Building Section

a new site awareness, contributes to the education of members of the surrounding community, and houses educators and researchers interested in this type of material and cultural history.

Las Ruinas also incorporates a gallery space; the double-height room would work as an exhibition and a social gathering/events space; it would become an entrance atrium for the academia. The gallery space was carefully planned to incorporate remains of the ruins on floor and wall surfaces. It would also integrate historic artifacts significant to the material culture of Boca de Nigua – including objects which would bring back a memory of the infamous slave rebellion.

Catering to the tourism industry, the proposal includes a spa adjacent to the building with the original "calderas." The spa, inspired by Roman baths of the Imperial Era, would include a Tepidarium (warm water), a Caldarium (hot water), and a Frigidarium (cold water). These variations of water temperatures allow for a diversity of spaces for contemplation and meditation.

View from trapiche

Ingenio Diego Caballero

The Ingenio Diego Caballero is located in one of the impressive slopes of San Cristóbal, near the small town of San Gregorio, west of the Nigua River. The Diego Caballero Sugar Mill squeezed the precious commodity of the sugarcane by means of hydraulic power. The Diego Caballero Sugar Mill was owned by Diego Caballero de la Rosa until 1538. This particular factory had a short life at its early beginnings: it was established in the second decade of the sixteenth century, began its decline around 1550, and was closed in 1580; nevertheless, it re-gained its productive success at some point in the mid-eighteenth century.

The remains of buildings can still be perceived in their original scale and grandiosity; particularly, one can still see the colossal proportions of the empty brick storage building at the top of the hill, the semicircular hydraulic water mill, and the complex carved-stone water ditches – which act as scars of infrastructure on the gentle slopes of the hill. At the bottom of the hill, one can also perceive the brick wall remnants of what used to be a boiler house. There are also other ruins covered by vegetation which, by pure speculation and on the basis of archaeological remains, can be understood as kilns, warehouses, and water tanks.

In addition to stories of slavery and emancipation, the location of the Ingenio Diego Caballero has a particular place in the political history of the Dominican Republic and the plans for the assassination of President Rafael Trujillo, in 1961. Like Boca de Nigua, the Diego Caballero Sugar Mill is also a UNESCO Monument for the Patrimony of Humanity since 2002.

Ingenio Diego Caballero

Laura Beltran & David Holmes

Built within the ruins of the Ingenio de Diego Caballero sugar mill, the project is a hotel composed of seven commemorative towers. These seven unique towers pay tribute to those who lost their lives on or near this site while performing a mission to assassinate the former presidential dictator Rafael Trujillo.

Each unique tower consists of five stories with one room per floor. The facades represent the individuality of each one of the seven people executed in 1961. The façades are built of white concrete; wooden louvres protect the small windows from the strength of the Dominican sun. Each room contains a balcony to appreciate the astounding views of the natural scenery, the nearby Caribbean Sea, and the courtyards below.

On each tower, the ground level is wide open – with the exception of stairs and elevators. The building body rests on pilotis; this modern device allows to experience the 260 foot length of the foundation of the ruins without being interrupted by any type of building footprints. Among the cluster of towers there are six unique 20 ft. x 20 ft. courtyards (a void representing the same width and length of the towers).

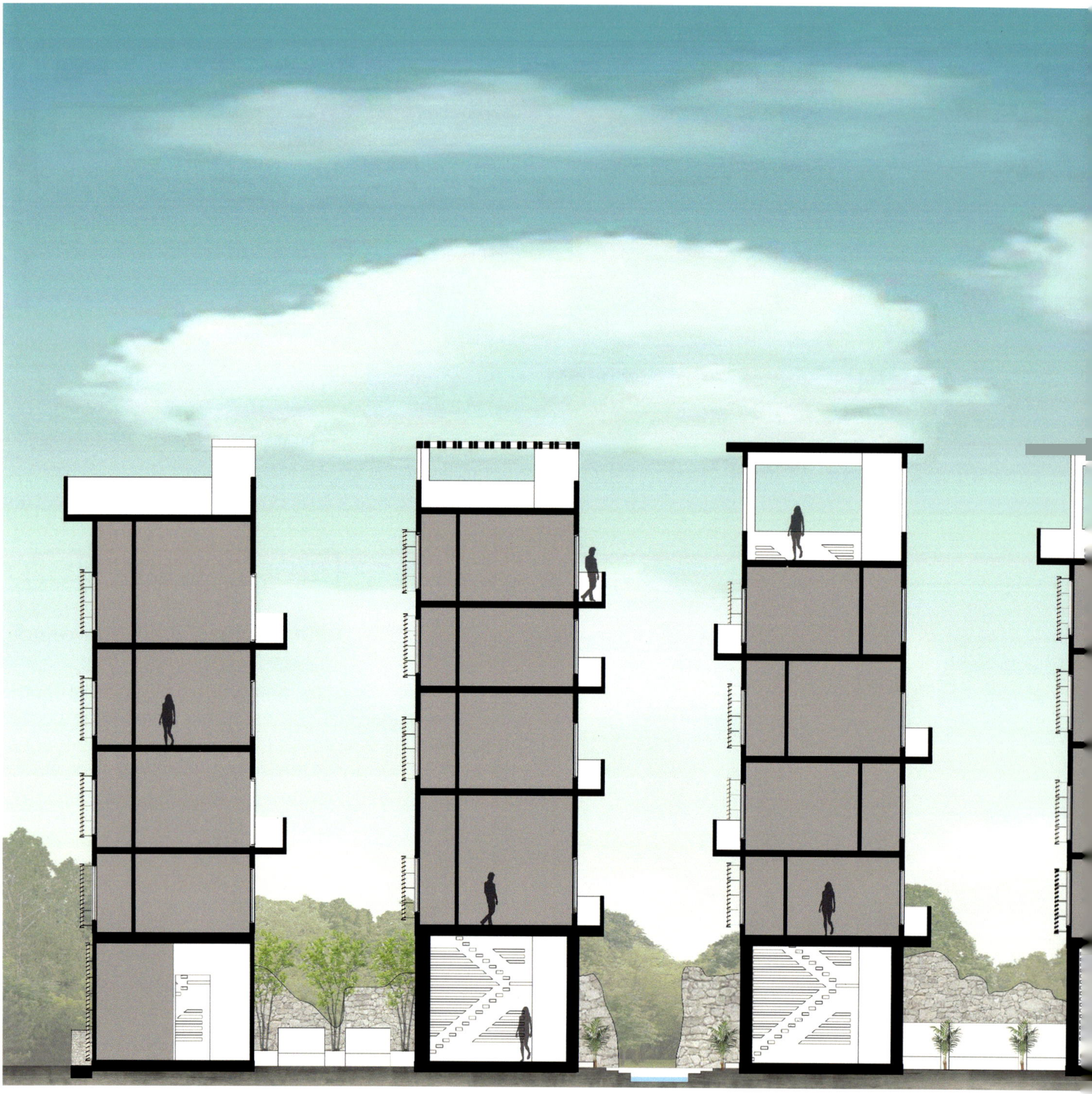

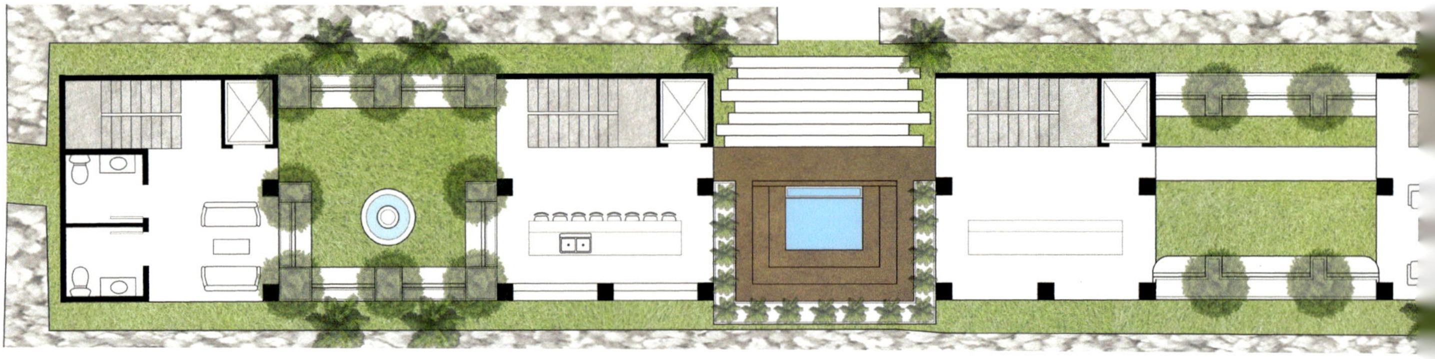

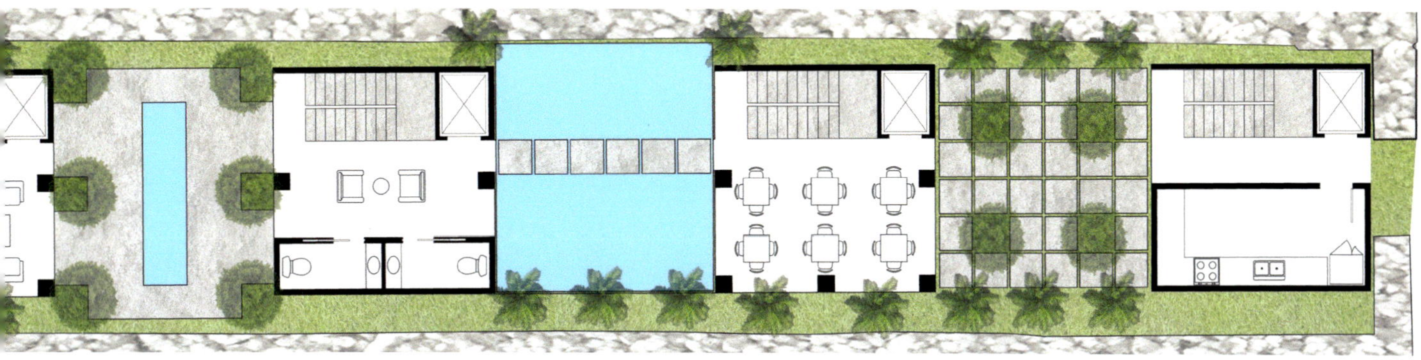

These open spaces serve as outdoor recreational sitting rooms for the guests staying at the hotel. The top floor of each tower has a unique terrace space for guests to enjoy views of the Caribbean Sea and the city of Santo Domingo skyline up the coast.

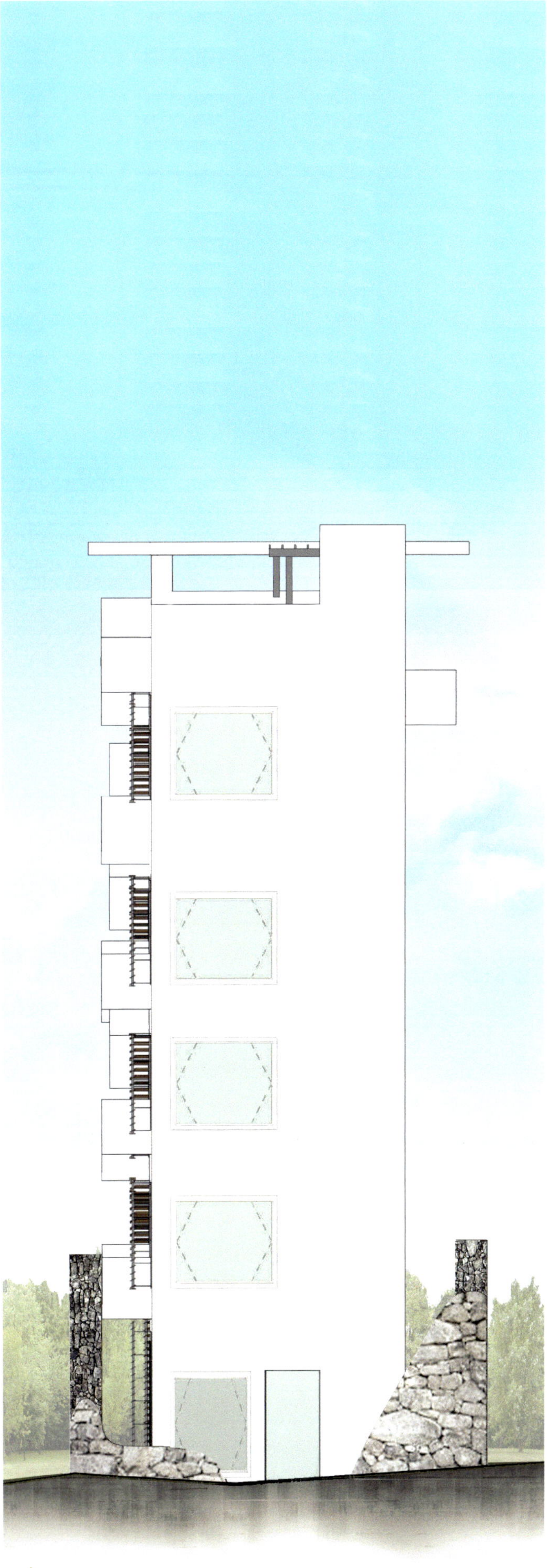

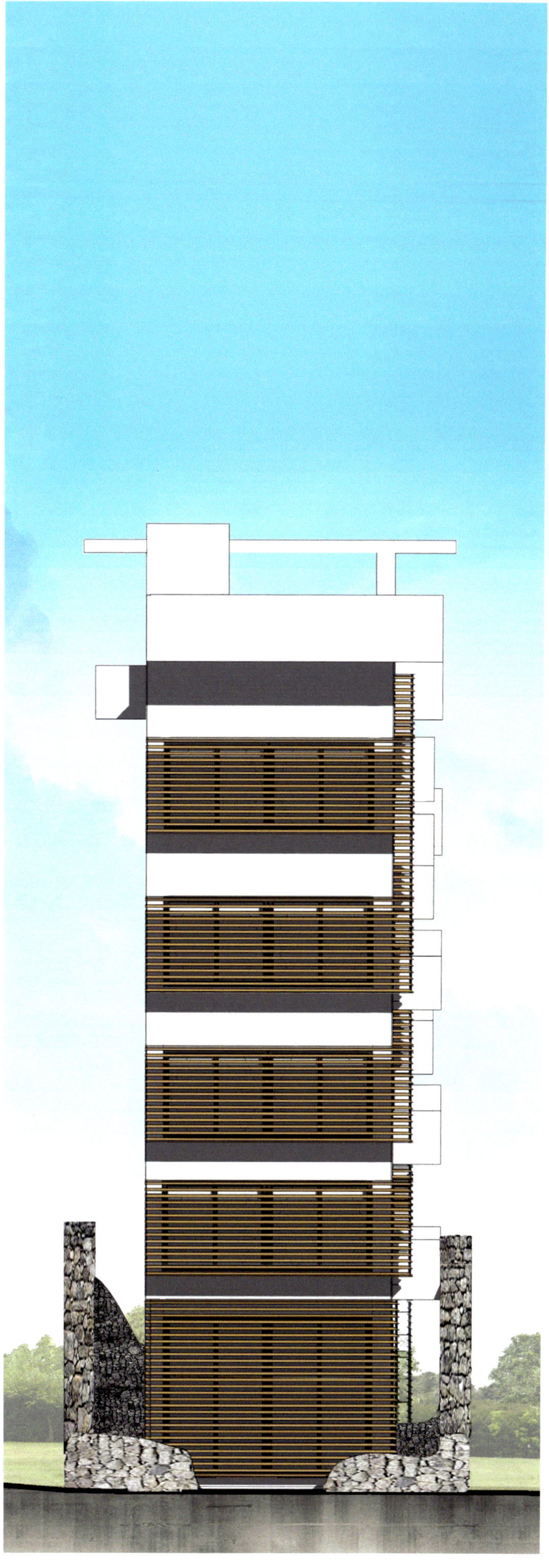

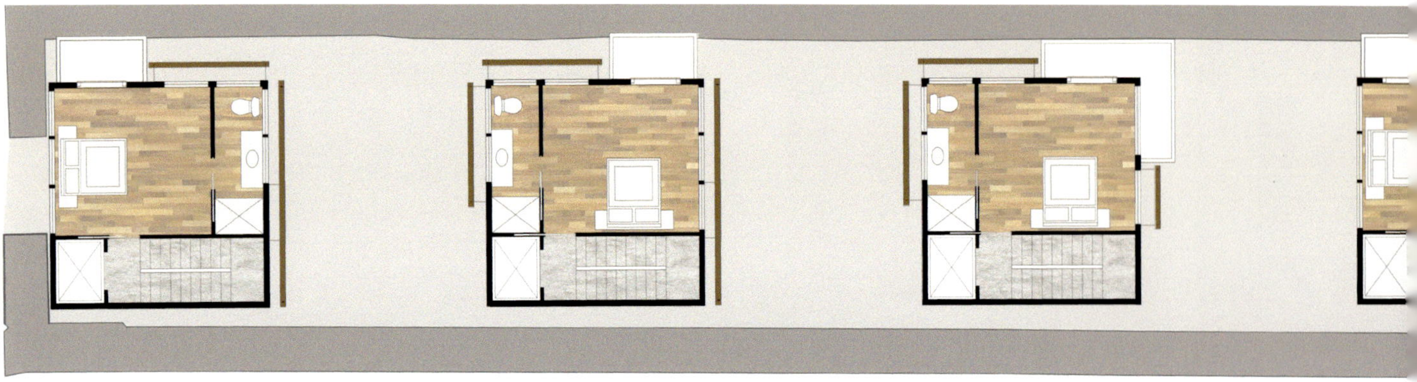

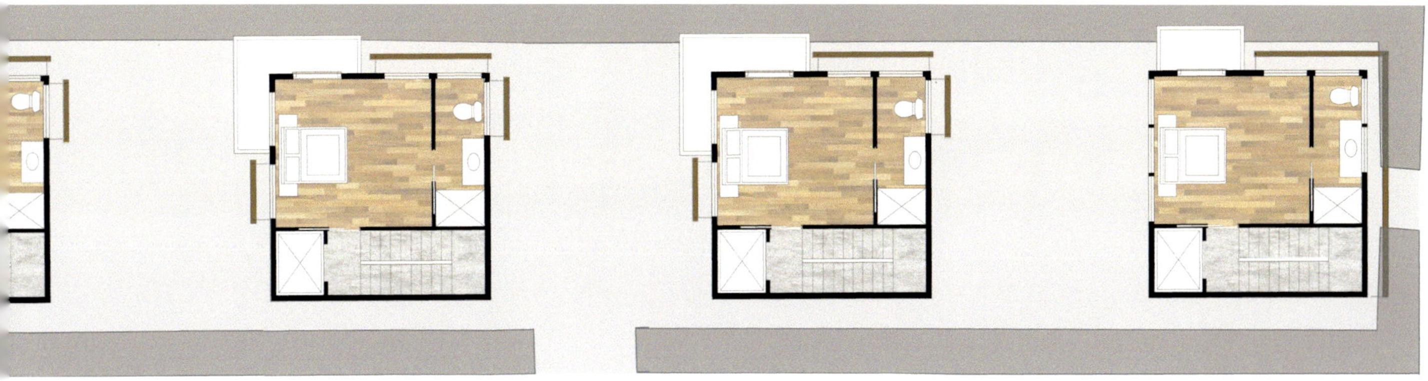

Ingenio Diego Caballero

Michael Burke & Israel Martinez

Inserted underneath the existing ruins and topography, this project proposed for the site of Ingenio Diego Caballero consists of a main hotel; the structure is initially perceived as a concrete platform until guests approach its subterranean interior to have an opportunity to overlook the tropical site foliage.

Ingenio Diego Caballero is one of the sugar mills with the least amount of preserved ruins on site; proposing the main hotel to be constructed underneath the ground enabled the old to not be overpowered and covered by the new. Additionally, this proposal adds ten huts surrounding the existing ruins at the foot of the mountain – not too far away from the main hotel. The hut consists of a main structure built in concrete with wooden louvers allowing for natural ventilation. Inside the huts there is a small kitchen, a bathroom, a living room, and a mezzanine bedroom with a double bed.

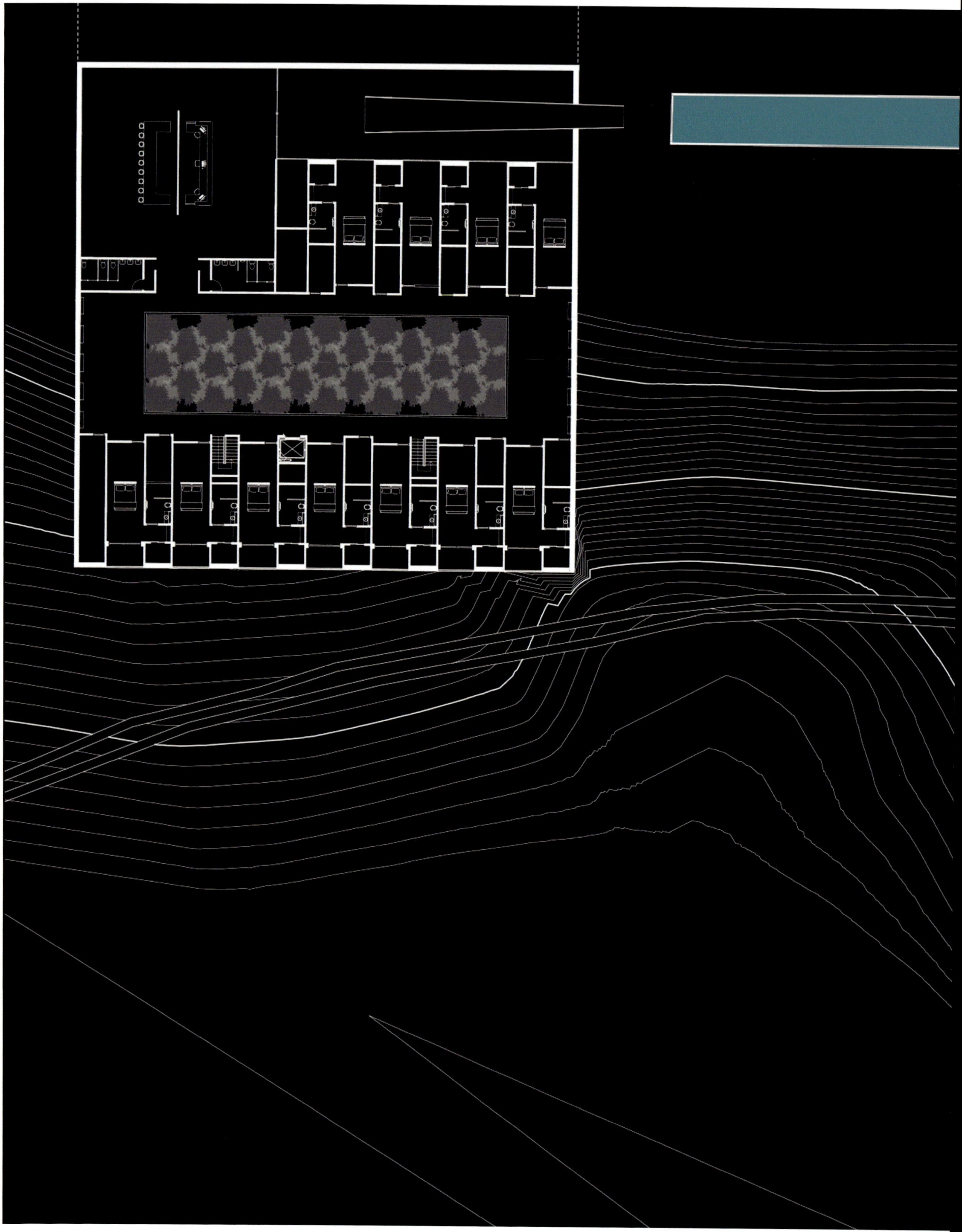

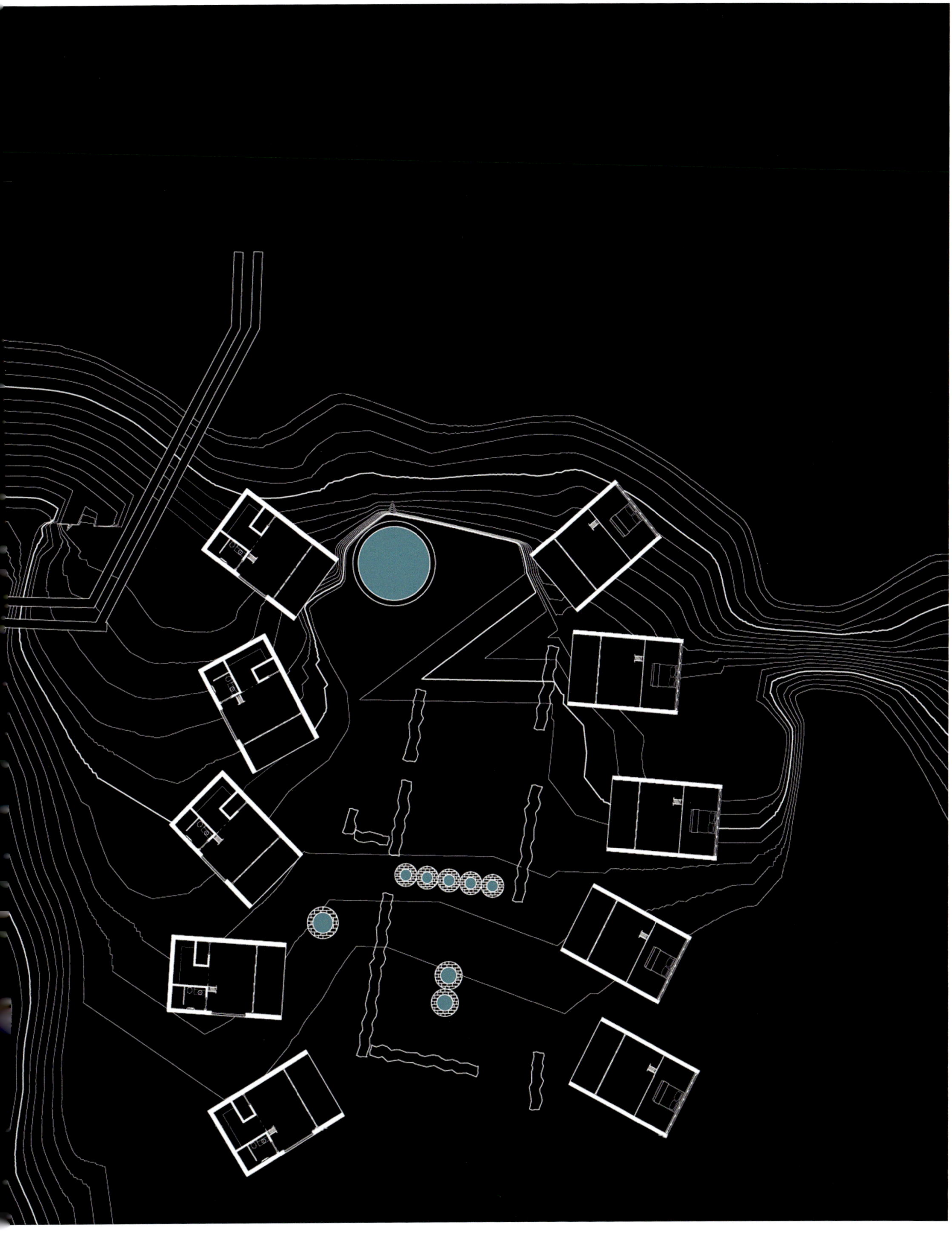

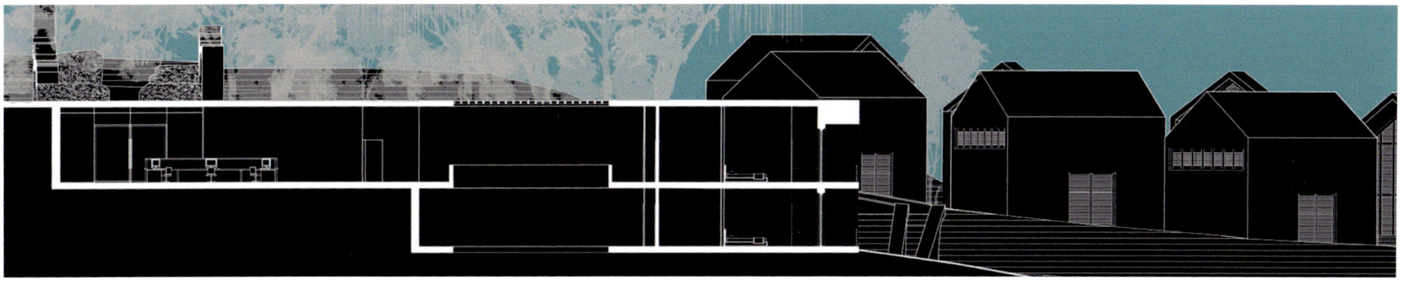

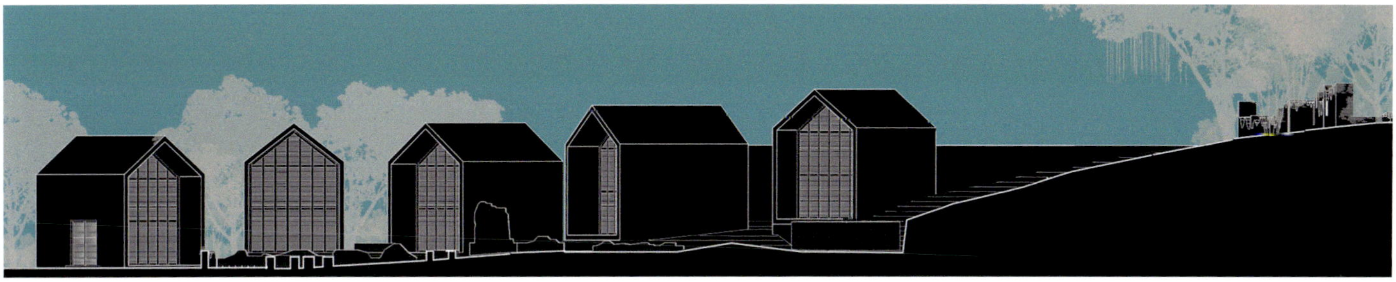

Ingenio Palave

Although these are also vestiges of a sad moment in the human history of the Caribbean, the ruins of the so-called Ingenio Palave do not provide precise evidence of an overall sugar mill complex; in this case, the facilities associated with a typical sugarcane production site have not been found and the only actual ruins are those of what seems to be the house of a slave master at the top of a cliff. Unlike the other three sugar mills sites in this study, the so-called Ingenio Palave remains a mysterious example in the area of speculative archaeology.

The slave master's mansion is placed at the highest point of a gentle sloping hill with a semi-circular clearing along its front façade and a forest in the back; the back of the site has a deep cliff which, as speculated by historians, could have been the place for the type of hydraulic sugar mill which is typical in the Dominican Republic.

The front façade has a symmetrical composition with two tower-like structures on the sides and a deep adorned loggia in the middle; nevertheless, the rear façade breaks the overall symmetry of the composition when the building removes a room on the second floor to provide the bottom floor with one single sweeping roof of two rooms in length. This is a typical 3x2 composition with wooden rods approximately 16.5 feet in width.

Ingenio Palave

Sol Perchik & Andrea Szapiro

Palave Cultural Center for the Arts brings educational and interactive programs to the surrounding neighborhoods. The interior of the existing historic ruins is restored, while three steel towers provide unique exhibition halls for the display of cultural objects/art/documents related to the history of sugar mills in the Dominican Republic.

A wrap-around extension building creates an outdoor plaza with an imposing amphitheater for the gathering of the local community or for special events.
The resulting space may be used by local actors and to project films for the entertainment of the community and visiting people alike.

The proposed extension of the existing building contains several workshop spaces for pottery, photography, painting, filmmaking, etc. These activities are proposed to invite people of all ages as well as to create a lively environment where once upon a time reigned the sugar industry of the Dominican Republic and its culture of slavery.

Current page, Site plan of project

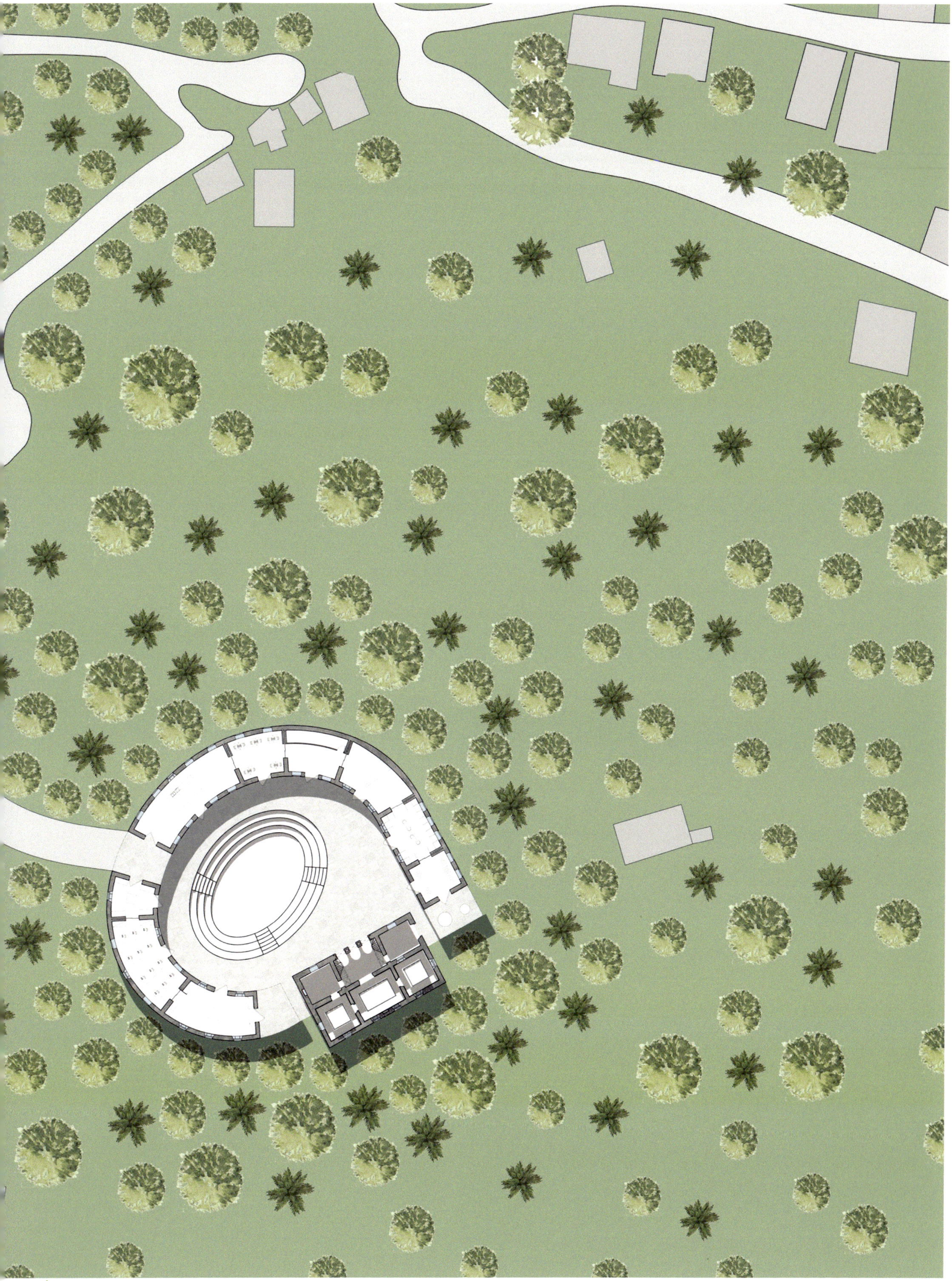

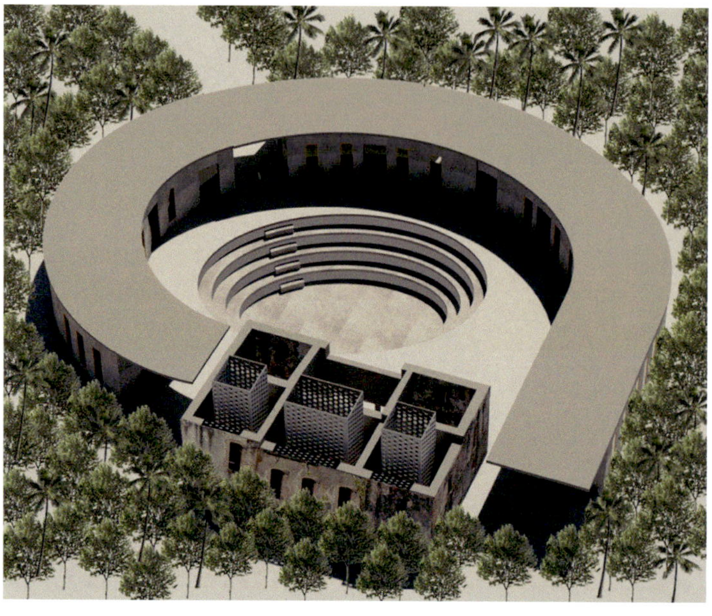

Ingenio Palave

Abdulaziz Alghannam & Luis Felipe Delgado

This proposal stabilizes the structure and keeps the ruins of the original mansion in their existing conditions. Instead of a project of historic preservation on the basis of a mysterious past filled with ambiguities, this project opts for the creation of a community center, marketplace, and school house at the core of the informal settlement surrounding the site.

The entrance to the complex is conically shaped to exaggerate the perspective and to increase the perceptual scale of the mansion. It provides a paved plaza with a retail market hub with six stalls on one side and an open Greek Stoa-like space on the other. Seven pavilions, with their unique architectural characteristics, surround a new semi-circular space facing the existing ruins. The pavilions are joined by a continuous roof structure which serves as a terrace for the classroom spaces above and below.

The ruins are meant to remain intact to serve as potential historic preservation material for the training of craftsmen specialized in the restoration of historic monuments.

Current page, site plan of project. *Previous page,* aerial view

Ingenio Engombe

The Ingenio Engombe was built sometime between 1533 and 1536. It is one of the most important and complete sugar mill examples in the Dominican industrial heritage of colonial times. The area of the ruins is approached via a narrow road within an existing community; it is nowadays located in the outskirts of the metropolitan area of the City of Santo Domingo.

The Engombe Sugar Mill complex occupies about 1500 acres of land along the Rio Haina and, as usual in Dominican Sugar Mills, it is placed on a gently sloping site with an informal landscape enclosing the production complex.

The sugar mill complex was occupied by approximately 20 Spanish residents and 120 slaves. It consists of a two-story slave master house, a small chapel, a warehouse, a slave shed, a typical semi-circular "trapiche" powered by both water and horses (not oxen), and scattered remains of what is believed to be slave accommodations and additional residences for the Spanish population.

The large two-story house, known as "Palacio de Engombe," and the single nave chapel stand among the collection of buildings and ruins in this property. Both structures were built in stone. During the chapel restoration of 1963, the roof that had collapsed around 1930 was rebuilt.

In his book *The architectural monuments of Hispaniola*, art historian Erwin Walter Palm points out that the chapel in the Ingenio Engombe was originally dedicated to Santa Ana. According to him, "this chapel was the only religious construction in the sixteenth century that did not include Gothic style details – common in early churches and convents in the colonial period". In 1972 and 1999, archaeological surveys were carried out in selected areas with the aim of locating some structures and collecting vital samples for understanding the site. However, the information is still insufficient and more extensive research is needed to define the uses of the remains that were part of the mill and how it worked.

Ingenio Engombe

Andrea Hernandez & Emily Suarez

The Dominican Republic sugar industry has a very dark history. Engombe is, like all other sugar mills in the Dominican Republic, tied to the pain and suffering of the people who worked there. Throughout the years, the slave stories, within the narrative of "the Other," have almost been forgotten. At Engombe, as in many other places in the Dominican Republic, slaves did not have a name, they were just a numbered commodity.

This project is meant to exhibit the life of the slave, even if it means showcasing the unpleasant past required to commemorate the life and humanness of those people who, in contemporary culture, are much more than just numbers.

Adapting the existing sugar mill is a layered project with strong ties to the social infrastructure and history of the site. The Engombe site is in the middle of a community near the Haina River. The site has four main buildings: the mansion, the stable, the church , and the mill. The main axis of the project is centered around the stable. Everything is developed around the stable because that's where the motor/life of the sugar mill was; that was the place where slaves worked – the true heart of the site.

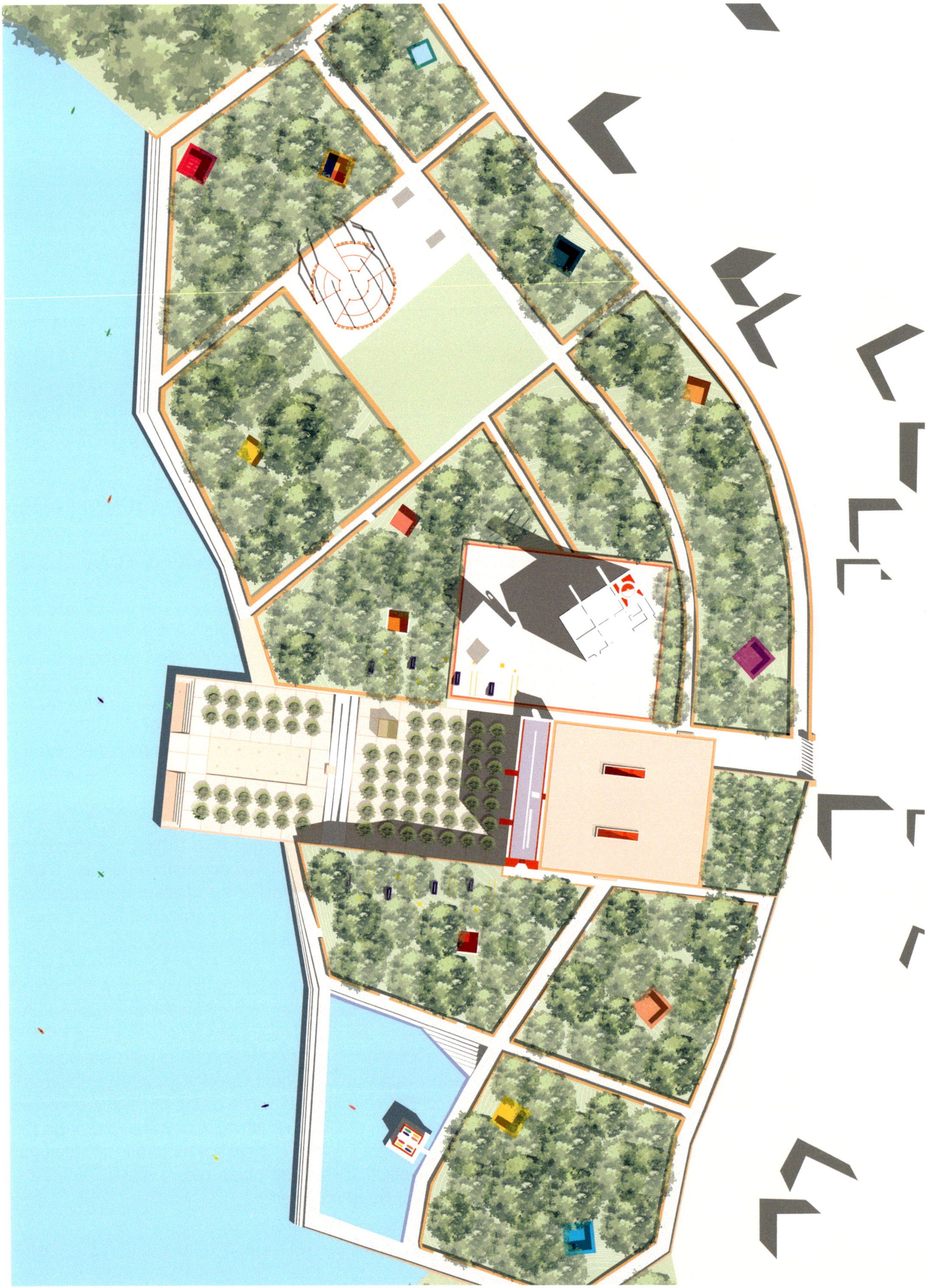

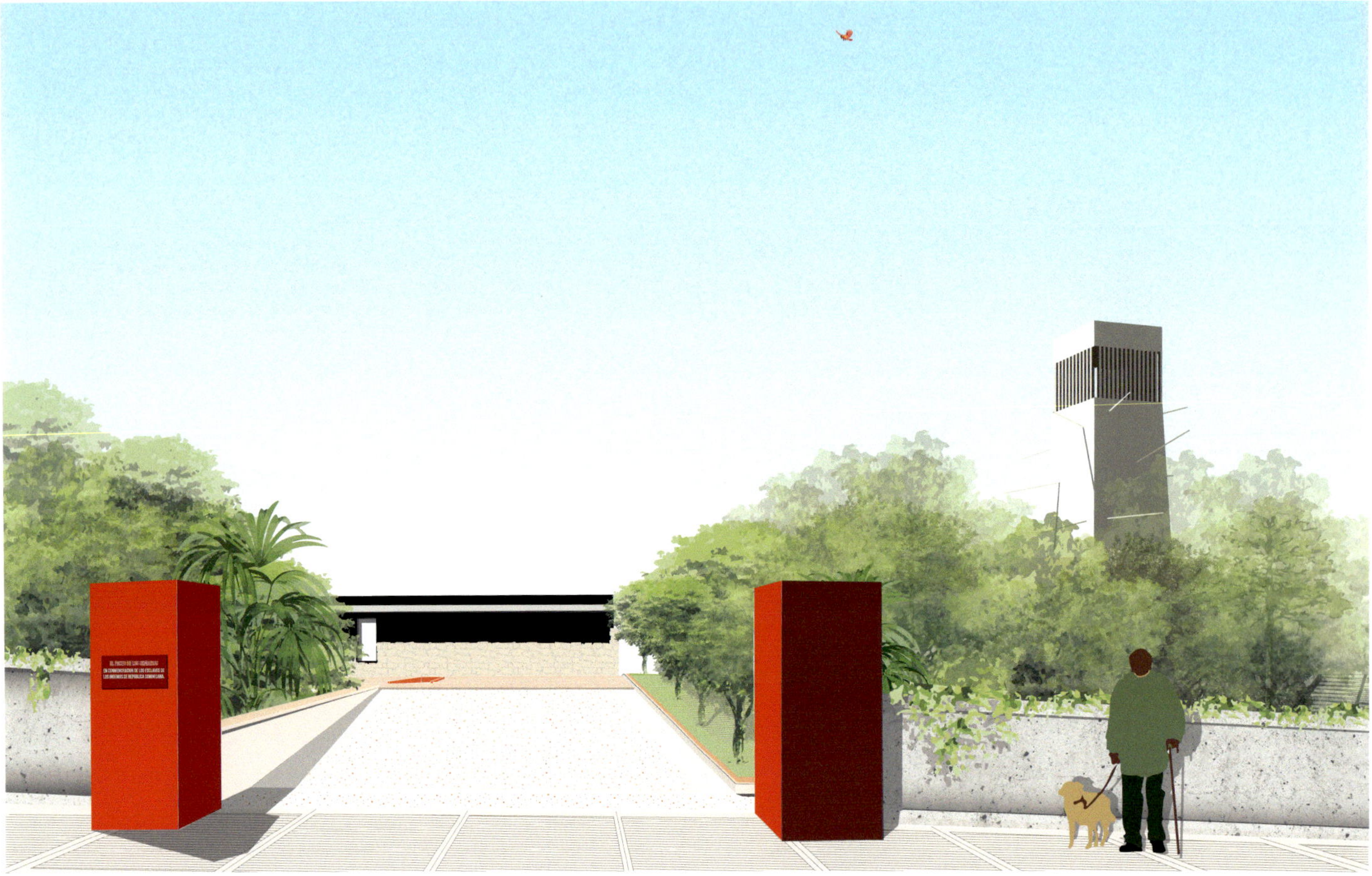

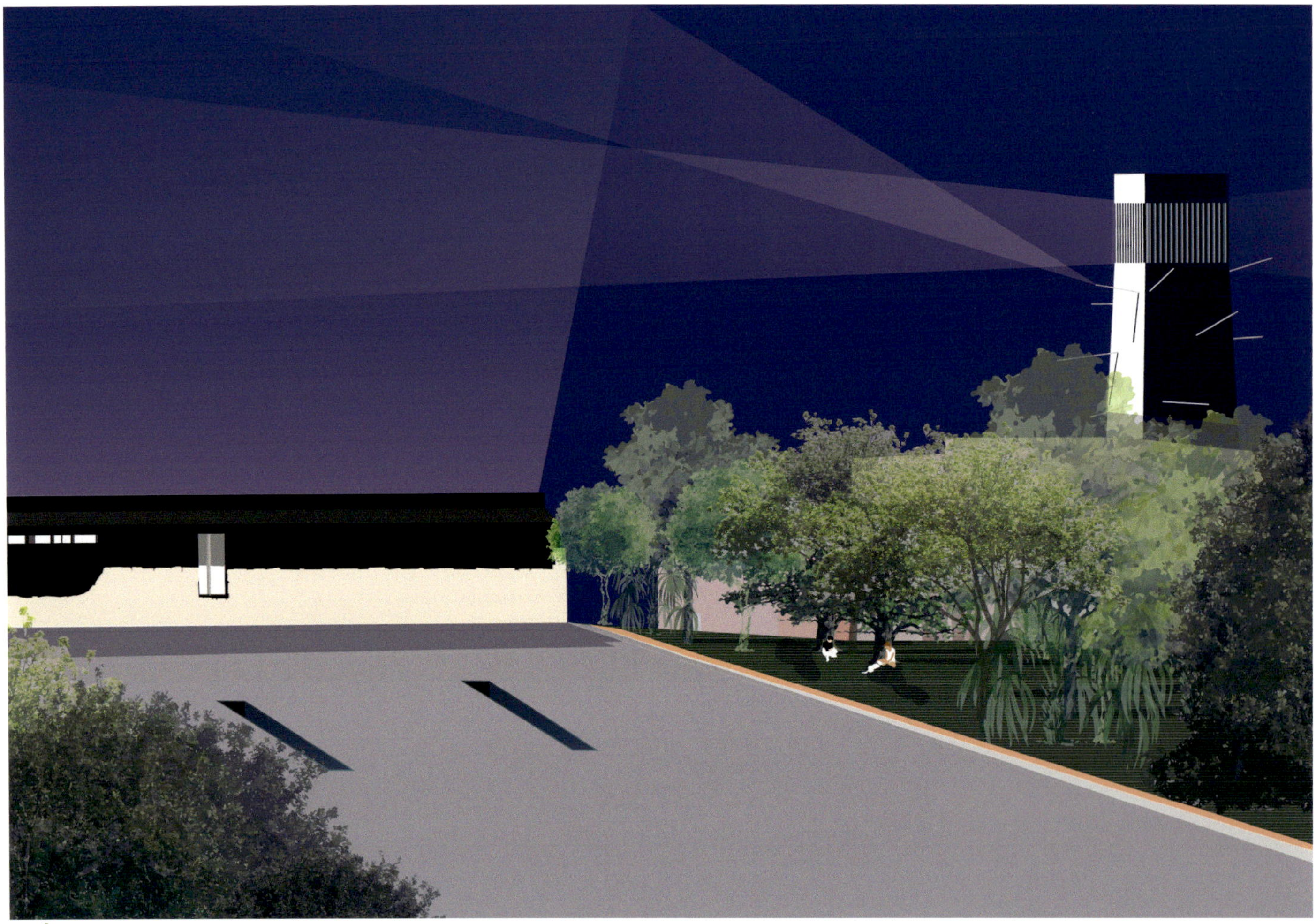

This proposal wants to represent and create awareness around the former social injustices happening in the mill as well as around the complicated relationship between white men and their numbered slaves. As the heart of the site, the stable is renovated to become a sensorial museum, a horizontal entity that symbolizes the former oppression. The master's mansion, even though secondary to the project, is turned into a whitewashed watch tower with 16 telescopes pointed to the most important mills in the Dominican Republic. The whitewashed tower stands as a lookout landmark – as if it were guarding this site. The last building is the Mill itself – the place where the sugar was produced; the proposal makes a subtle intervention with a vertical garden over, under, and inside its physical remains.

This is a layered project. One of its most important aspects is the connection of the buildings on the site. The Engombe sugar mill is in the middle of a community and, as such, it has become the most important public infrastructure in the region. In that manner, the proposed trail is treated not only as a connector of the site buildings, but also as a public program. The paths were treated in materials like cobblestone to unite the whole site with some sort of unifying theme. A variety of benches protrude from the ground and slice the site into smaller areas.

All paths lead to the water's edge of the Haina River – a local river that connects all the mills together at some point or another. The condition of the water edge became an opportunity for the creation of a lively place. Such water-edge axis was marked by a "deep scar" in the land on the south side of the stable. This "deep scar" was counterposed to the stable as the building/space with utmost importance; it placed the stable on a sort of high pedestal, where visitors would have an opportunity to admire the original building. In the lower plaza/space a new program includes restaurants carved into the original topography. These restaurants face each other, with the plaza as a facilitator of this contrast. The restaurants have skylights providing their interiors with indirect natural light.

A special attention to detail was paid when the new was represented with a new material to differentiate it from the old. The restoration and repair of the site was driven by the idea that the original structure should be emphasized in its spatial context and original materiality. This proposal is based on the following statement by David Chipperfield: "the new must reflect the old without imitating it".

Ingenio Engombe

Maxwell Erickson & Olivia Kramer

This mill comprised a trapiche for the milling of sugar cane, with an attached furnace room, an open-air structure with stone columns and a thatch roof, a drying building, of which only a small fragment of one wall remains, a warehouse for storing the finished product before shipment, which still has three of its original walls, a church, which has been reconstructed, and an owners' mansion, which has also received restoration work.

At a macro level, to address locals' needs for increased safety, connectivity, and awareness, a proposed local ferry system will connect the site to neighboring communities and Palave, and a walking/biking trail along the river's edge will provide a recreational opportunity, supported by small station buildings holding first aid, bicycle repair supplies, and snacks. A boathouse inspired by vernacular Dominican architecture sits on the water's edge, with a ferry pier and covered boat slips at the water level. A restaurant/bar and a multipurpose education/event space sit above this area, opening to a wraparound porch. An observation tower, inspired by Angiolo Mazzoni's water towers at Termini station in Rome, features a staircase winding around a core of louvers. This structure ties into an interactive aerial walkway system, with stations in strategic locations along the route with educational signage teaching the history of the site while providing overhead views of the ruins.

The warehouse has a new glass and translucent polycarbonate structure sitting within its stone walls and serves as an Italian-style coffee bar/ café, library, and reception space. Books line the outer walls, and built-in benches inspired by those at the cloister of Santa Maria Della Pace in Rome frame narrow windows in the historic walls.

Anchored by the reception space, in the warehouse, is a proposed eco-hotel of 12 cabins. Inspired by Peter Zumthor's Zinc Mine Museum in Norway, the cabins are nestled in the trees, situated to capture views of the river, and raised on stilts, allowing the forest floor to run unabated underneath them. Their design allows breezes to flow around all sides of the cabin to keep occupants cool. Inside each cabin there is a full kitchen, informal dining, and loft bedroom overlooking a two-story living space that opens out to a deck with a view of the river.

This project keeps the historic church, playfield, and mansion untouched, as these spaces continue being enjoyed by the community.

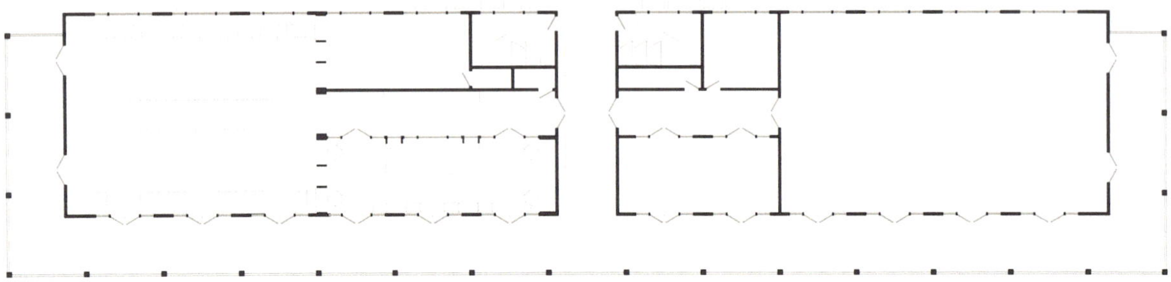

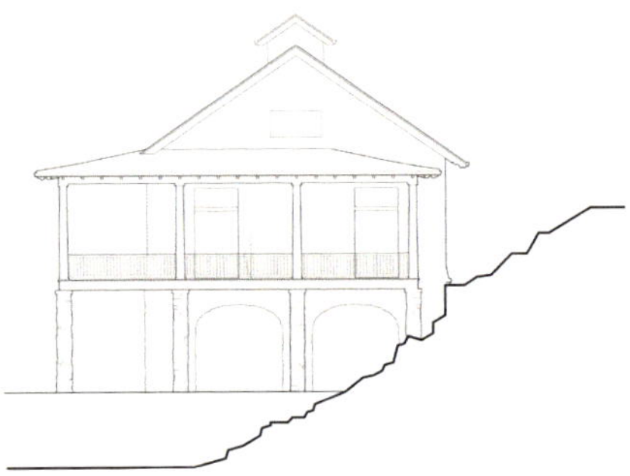

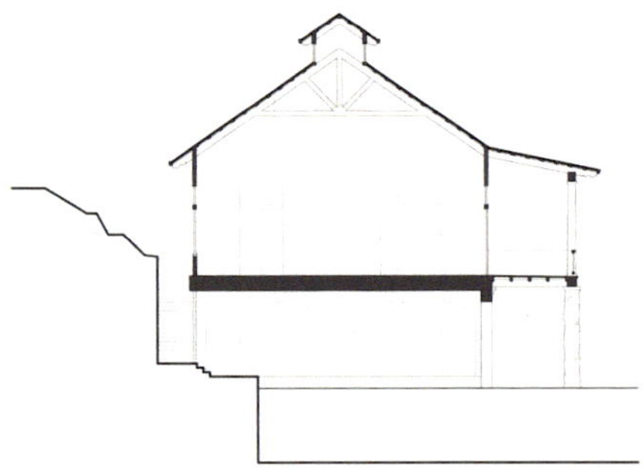

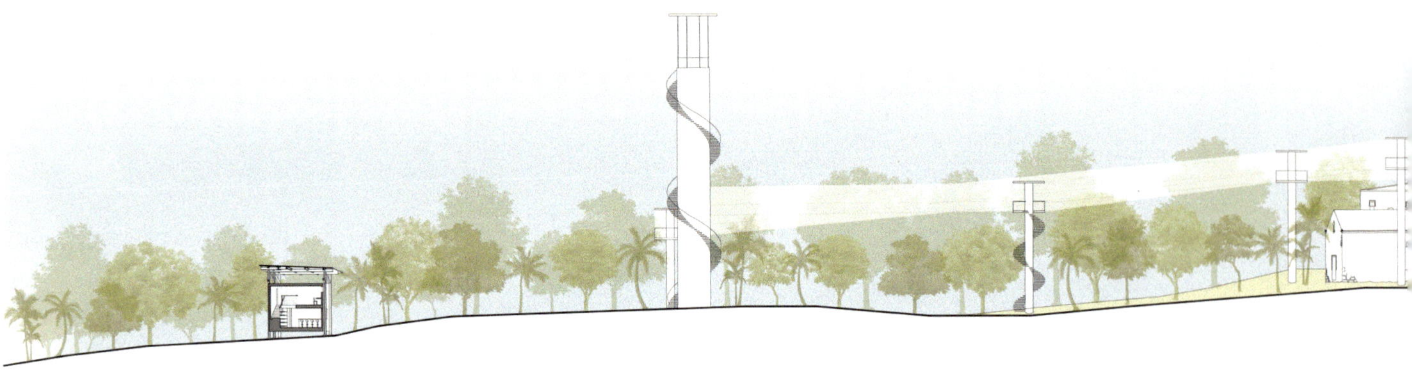

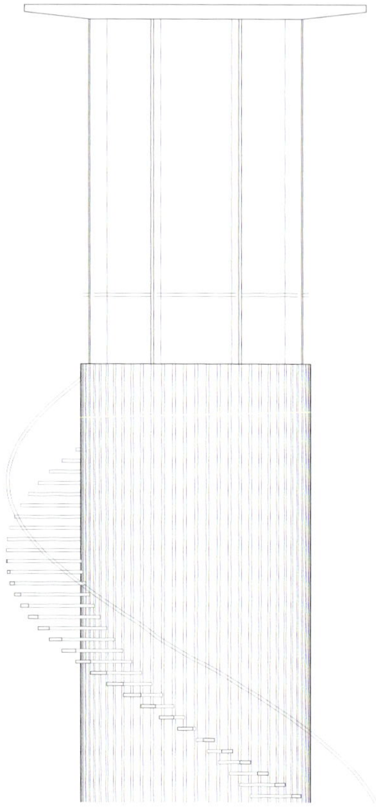

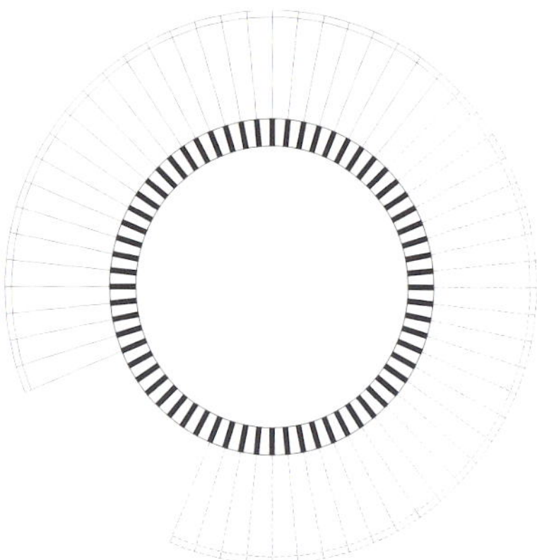

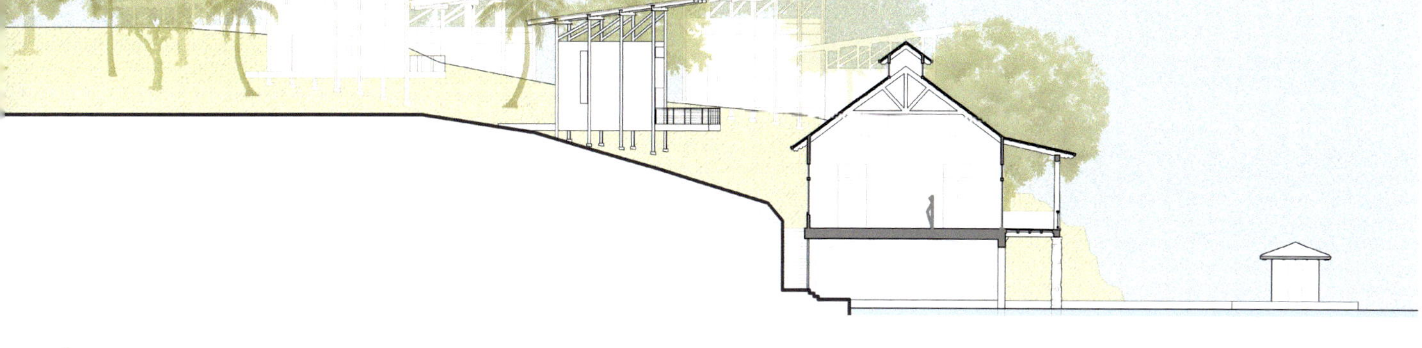

ACKNOWLEDGMENTS

This design studio would have been impossible to achieve without the generous financial and intellectual contribution of the Canin Family. Although Brian and Myrna Canin were not able to visit the Dominican Republic because of conflicting business appointments, they attended every review and, with their comments and gentle demeanor, motivated us to advise students, critique their work, and produce the beautiful projects in the pages of this book.

As usual, Dean Rodolphe el-Khoury, at the School of Architecture of the University of Miami, was our greatest cheerleader and promoter. He has had a special affection for the Dominican Republic and went overboard to make sure that a studio of this caliber would produce outstanding results in this area of the Caribbean. His challenge to us to produce this book has been the grounding reason for all our efforts.

We also want to credit the enormous patience demonstrated by our close family members. We think that, by now, they probably understand that when we go away for a few days we are not just having fun in the traditional superficial way; we are having fun doing important research on cities, buildings, and historic landscapes, immersing ourselves in foreign cultures and places, and attempting to understand our multiple professional roles as teachers, intellectuals, architects, preservationists, artists, and urban designers. We are very lucky to have them in our lives. And, we are even luckier when we realize how much we love what we do.

Finally, there would be no projects without students and, in this case, our students stepped up to the provocation of adapting themselves to the pre-conditions of a different cultural medium and challenged our notions of appropriateness in historic preservation, adaptive reuse, the nature of time, the conventions of newness and modernity, the ideas of beauty and congruency, and the true essence of architecture, urbanism, landscape architecture, and interior design.

CREDITS

We would like to acknowledge some of our professional project collaborators as well as those who offered their insight and knowledge of these unique sites.

UNPHU Coordinators

Omar Rancier Dean of the School of Art and Architecture
Heydi de Moya Director of Undergraduate Program
Aldo Erazo Director of International Relations
Jose Constanzo Upper level studio faculty
Miguel Rodriguez Upper level studio faculty
Juan Mubarak Upper level studio faculty

Tour of Zona Colonial led by

Virginia Flores Restoration Architect
Esteban Prieto Restoration Architect
Jorge Marte Architect and professor

Sugar Mills site visits led by

Mizoocki Mota Professor
Danilo Solano Architect
Santiago Duval Archaeologist

Hotel Billini Zona Colonial

Rosadela Serulle Manager

Direccion Nacional de Patrimonio Monumental

Edda Grullón Director
Annabel Hiraldo Architect

Students from the University of Miami School of Architecture

Sol Perchik
Andrea Szapiro
Luis Felipe Delgado
Abdulaziz Alghannam
Andrea Hernandez
Emily Suarez
Maxwell Erickson
Olivia Kramer
Daniella Cancel
Daniella Huen
Adrianna Rivera
Catalina Chaves
Laura Beltran
David Holmes
Michael Burke
Israel Martinez

HISTORIC SUGARMILLS IN SANTO DOMINGO, Case Studies in Adaptive Reuse.

Published in the United States of America

Book design by Daniella Cancel and Maria A. Cannavó V.

30 29 28 27 26 25   6 5 4 3 2 1

The Library of Congress Control Number: 2024913617

ISBN 979-8-218-45072-4

The Brian Canin Urban Design Award
University of Miami School of Architecture
1223 Dickinson Drive
Coral Gables, FL 33146